I BECAME INSANE, WITH
LONG INTERVALS OF HORRIBLE
SANITY.
EDGAR ALLAN POE

Nevermore

THE HAUNTED LIFE AND
MYSTERIOUS DEATH OF
EDGAR ALLAN POE

Troy Taylor

AN AMERICAN HAUNTINGS INK BOOK

This Book is Published By:
American Hauntings Ink
Jacksonville, Illinois | 217.791.7859
Visit us on the Internet at http://www.americanhauntingsink.com

978-1-7352706-5-4
First Edition - April 2021

Printed in the United States of America

Table of Contents

Part One

Part Two

Rain was falling on Baltimore on the afternoon of October 3, 1849, but this didn't stop Joseph Walker, who worked for the *Baltimore Sun*, from walking over to Ryan's Tavern, a public house on Fell's Point. It was Election Day, and the inn was crowded and festive. The public house served as a polling location for the 4th Ward polls.

Walker crossed the street, heading for the entrance, when he noticed a man lying in the gutter outside. This was not out of the ordinary - not in this part of the city and certainly not on Election Day - but something about the man caught his eye. He seemed to be delirious, and he was wearing a mismatched collection of second-hand clothes. The man was barely conscious and was unable to move, or even lift his head. As Walker stepped closer, he realized that he knew the man - it was the poet, Edgar Allan Poe.

Now concerned, he stopped and asked Poe if he had any acquaintances in Baltimore that might be able to help him. Poe gave Walker the name of Joseph

Snodgrass, a magazine editor, and a friend with some medical training. Walker immediately went into the pub and dashed off a letter to be delivered to Snodgrass, asking for help. He explained where Poe was and that he said he was acquainted with Snodgrass. He noted that Poe was in great distress and added, "he is in need of immediate assistance."

Poe was carried inside the pub and placed in a chair, where Snodgrass found him a short time later. Though warned the poet was not in good condition, the sight of him gave Snodgrass a shock. He was wearing cheap, dirty, torn clothing that - as it would turn out - was not his own.

It was later discovered that Poe had left Richmond, Virginia one week earlier, bound for Philadelphia, and was not seen again until Walker discovered him in the gutter outside the pub.

He remained unconscious for the next four days, finally dying on October 7. He never provided an explanation about how he ended up unconscious on the streets of Baltimore, wearing another man's clothing, and completely incoherent. Instead, he spent his last days suffering from fits of delirium and hallucinations.

On the night before his death, according to his attending physician, Poe repeatedly called out for "Reynolds" - a man who, to this day, remains a mystery.

Perhaps it is fitting that the death of the man regarded as the "father of the American mystery" remains shrouded in mystery after all these years.

What happened to Poe after he vanished and then reappeared in a stupor a few days later? Where did his clothing come from and who had it belonged to? Who was the mysterious "Reynolds" that he whispered of with his dying breaths?

Even Poe's life - and afterlife - is filled with mystery.

Did the man who spent his life writing of gruesome death once commit the brutal murder of a young woman, and create a crime that has never been solved?

And perhaps strangest of all, does Poe haunt the mysterious graveyard where his body is buried? And who is the stranger that appears at Poe's grave each year on the anniversary of his birth, leaving roses and cryptic messages behind?

During his lifetime, Poe crafted an image of himself as a man of mystery. Unappreciated in America during his lifetime, Poe's greatest literary fame was achieved in Europe. He was always penniless but played the part of a Southern gentleman. He had a drinking problem, but was enormously defensive about his background and talent and often rewrote his life history to suit the moment or his mood at the time. He married his thirteen-year-old cousin and lived with her and her mother and yet carried on "romances" with several other women while still married. After a period of insane grief, he asked three other women to marry him within a month of his wife's death from tuberculosis.

By his own request, the executor and editor of his final writings was a man that he disliked and who returned the sentiment by distorting and fabricating Poe's biography to the extent that much of the writer's life will always be a puzzle. Some believe that Poe knew this would happen, and eventually, had the last laugh. By allowing himself to be slandered in the way that he was, he created a controversy that has kept his name and his writings alive to this day.

His final five days of life are a blank slate. Even after more than 170 years of detective work, no one knows for sure what happened to Poe before he was found delirious on the streets of Baltimore.

Does Poe's spirit still walk because of all these lingering mysteries? There are many who believe this and if he does still walk in the old Baltimore cemetery where he was laid to rest, he probably does not walk there alone.

Even long after his death, we still don't have the answers to the mystery that was Edgar Allan Poe.

PART ONE:
A HAUNTED LIFE

1. A Mystery is Born

"I THINK THAT I HAVE ALREADY HAD MY SHARE OF TROUBLE FOR ONE SO YOUNG."
EDGAR ALLAN POE

Poe certainly did have his share of trouble. It practically started at his birth and continued throughout a life that was as strange and haunted as the tales that he concocted from his imagination.

David Poe, Edgar's father, planned a career in law until he met a young actress named Eliza Arnold, who was appearing on stage in Norfolk, Virginia. Smitten by her, he abandoned his legal studies and became a stage performer, much to his father's chagrin. David eventually joined Eliza's theatrical troupe, where he won over the recently widowed actress.

Eliza was only 19 at the time but she had already been an actress for 10 years. She was a celebrated beauty but only one known portrait of her exists. It shows a young woman with a round, fragile face and large eyes that are framed by dangling curls. Reviews often mentioned her "sweet melodious voice" and her "interesting figure."

Edgar's mother, Eliza Poe

David Poe was also apparently pleasing to look at, but his abilities as an actor left much to be desired. A critic wrote in 1806 - the year David and Eliza married - "the lady was young and pretty, and evinced talent both as singer and actress; the gentlemen was literally nothing."

Nine months after the two were married, in January 1807, Eliza gave birth to a son, Henry. Two years later, on January 19, 1809, Edgar was born in a boarding house near the Boston Common, near where the troupe was performing.

By this time, the Poes' marriage was strained. David was resentful of his wife's success and had become hard-drinking and quick-tempered, especially after he was criticized for his acting skills. Once, he berated an audience from the stage, and on another occasion, learned where a theater critic lived and went to his home to take issue of the hostile review the man had written about him. As his behavior became more and more erratic, Eliza was left with the burden of providing for the family. She had to perform right up until the week that Edgar was born and then had to return to the stage two weeks later.

A third child, Rosalie, arrived the following year. By this time, Henry had been sent to live with his paternal grandparents, while Edgar and his little sister were left in the care of nursemaids, one of whom, according to a family friend, "fed them liberally with bread soaked in gin." She also administered laudanum - an opium-based painkiller - to keep them from crying.

In July 1811, David Poe finally abandoned his family. It had been a long time coming but it was still a shock to Eliza. David only lived another five months. He died alone, destitute, and forgotten. Eliza didn't live much longer. She contracted tuberculosis and died in Richmond, Virginia, on December 8, 1811, with her children at her side. Edgar was not quite three.

During their mother's final illness, Edgar and Rosalie had been cared for by kindly actor friends by the name of Usher, but the couple were unable to take custody of them permanently. Their maternal grandparents had died years earlier and David's parents, who already had custody of Henry, had suffered financial reverses that made it impossible for them to raise two additional children. A home was found for Rosalie with a Richmond family named MacKenzie and Edgar was taken into the home of a wealthy merchant, John Allan.

John Allan, Poe's foster father, who never officially adopted the young boy. Poe and Allan would go on to have a combative relationship that would end with Allan disowning his foster son.

He became the closest thing to a father that Poe would ever know. His wife, Frances, a nervous and frail woman, was too sickly to have children of her own. Allan was a Scottish immigrant who was known for his many acts of charity - and also for his hot temper and arrogance. It was later written of him, "Mr. Allan was a good man in his way. He was sharp and exacting, and with his long, hooked nose, and small keen eyes looking out from under shaggy eyebrows, he always reminded me of a hawk."

At the time, the Allans were extremely rich, and Allan owned a complex of offices and warehouses in Richmond's business district from which he brokered tobacco, fine goods, and services across America and Europe.

Poe's nervous and frail foster mother, Frances. After her death, the relationship between Allan and Poe would finally shatter.

Edgar had gone from a life of poverty and struggle to a new world of wealth and indulgence. The Allans lavished attention and money on their new ward and promised that he would be given a first-rate education that befitted a young gentleman. From the start, though, John Allan's benevolence came with conditions. He became Edgar's godfather but never formally adopted him. He did, however, add his family name to Edgar's as a kind of honorific.

The newly christened Edgar Allan Poe turned out to be a charming and precocious child, with many of the theatrical tendencies of his mother. Dinner guests were often treated to poetry performances from the young boy as he stood on the dining room table in stockinged feet and a velvet suit.

In 1815, Edgar accompanied his foster parents to England for five years while John Allan established a European branch of his company. When he took care of business, Edgar was enrolled in a series of excellent boarding schools and introduced to Allan's relatives in Scotland. Allan took visible pride in his ward's academic accomplishments and showered him with gifts and ensured he always had plenty of money. One of his instructors later wrote that Poe was "a quick and clever boy and would've been a very good boy if he had not been spoilt by his parents."

In 1820, the family returned to Richmond and Edgar, now 11, continued his schooling and was soon after to read Horace in Latin and Homer in Greek. He had fallen in love with writing and had notebooks filled with poems, some of them so accomplished that John Allan considered having them published. A schoolmaster once wrote of him, "His imaginative powers seemed to take precedence of all his other faculties."

Poe was also regarded as a fine athlete and a young man of reckless courage. At 15, he swam six miles of the James River against "the strongest tides ever known in the river," followed by a boat filled with cheering friends. Poe later bragged that this feat was equal to swimming 20 miles in still water and added, "I would not think much of attempting to swim the British Channel from Dover to Calais."

Despite his swagger, though, Poe was always a bit apart from his peers. He was remembered as sensitive and somewhat aloof but would "strain every nerve to oblige a friend."

As he grew older, he became keenly aware of his tenuous place in Richmond society. He was only the half-adopted son of a wealthy family; he had not been born into wealth. He was dependent on the generosity of his foster father and over time, that generosity had become increasingly uncertain. As Edgar got older and more willful, Allan's devotion began to wane. When he was angry, he often threatened to "turn the young man adrift." Poe was never allowed to lose sight of the fact that without Allan, he would have nothing.

Allan's failing charity was undoubtedly caused by a series of business problems that had dogged his return to Richmond. As his

Image of Poe as a young boy

Below: This image is believed to be a young Poe. It was discovered in 1905 and while it has not been authenticated, many experts believe that it's genuine.

financial status became more precarious, Poe's increasingly independent behavior struck him as being thankless. Allan complained in a letter, "The boy possesses not a spark of affection for us, not a particle of gratitude for all my care and kindness toward him."

Unsure of his position at home, Poe looked elsewhere for affection. He formed an intense attachment to Jane Standard, the mother of a classmate, whom he later recalled as "the first, purely ideal love of my soul." He visited her often, read his poetry aloud to her, and then reveled in her praise and encouragement. She was, Poe said, "an angel to my forlorn and darkened nature."

By all accounts, Jane was a beautiful and tragic woman, given to fits of melancholy, and illness. Poe watched with mountain despair as she slowly succumbed to a wasting disease. She was not yet 30-years-old when she died in April 1824, a few months after Edgar's 15th birthday. It was a stark reminder of his own mother's death years before and the loss of Jane Standard cut even more deeply because of it. A grief-stricken Edgar was often found mourning at her graveside, keeping a vigil with Jane's son, Robert.

Poe's deep grief over the death of Jane Standard widened the rift with John Allan, who saw his behavior as further evidence of his neglect for Allan and his wife. Poe, meanwhile, had found another recipient for his wild emotions. Less than a year after Jane's death, the forlorn young man fell in love with Sarah Elmira Royster, the 15-year-old daughter of one of the Allans' neighbors. Poe was aware that her father considered him an unsuitable match - mostly because of his questionable position in the Allan family - but Poe managed to persuade Sarah to agree to a secret engagement.

In March 1825, Allan's fortune was restored by an inheritance from a wealthy uncle. Financially secure for the first time in several years, he bought a luxurious new home on Main Street in Richmond that had a splendid view of the James River and the capitol building. Soon after, the University of Virginia opened its doors in Charlottesville, just 60 miles away. As Poe neared his 17th birthday, Allan made plans to enroll him there, both as a statement of his own wealth and position, and as a means of honoring the vow he'd made years before to provide the young man with a quality

Poe's former room in Range Hall has been preserved by the Raven Society on campus. We've been assured that it's not haunted.

education. Privately, Allan would be relieved to have his troublesome foster son out of the house and he hoped that college life would help to settle him.

In February 1826, Poe arrived in Charlottesville. Life at the new college was less than ideal. The students had to contend with the hardships of the university's ongoing construction, including crowded, cold buildings and questionable sanitation. There were, however, some impressive rewards. Thomas Jefferson, then 83-years-old, was the university's first rector and a fixture on campus. Poe dined with him on several occasions and was among the mourners when the former president died on July 4 of that year.

Poe was not the wild rebel among his classmates as some legends claim - at first anyway. Jefferson had designed the university with the sons of wealthy Virginia planters in mind. Believing these "spirituous fellows" would chafe at the kind of discipline required at Harvard or Yale, he established a code of behavior that set aside restrictive rules in favor of self-governance.

This experiment was not a success.

A student uprising occurred the first year, with books, bricks, and bottles of urine thrown at professors. In a letter home, Poe told John Allan that fights among students were "so trifling an occurrence" that no one even took notice of them. He went on to describe one noteworthy brawl during which a student, having been struck in the head by a rock, "drew a pistol - which are all the fashion here - and had it not missed fire would have put an end to the controversy."

In this kind of atmosphere, Poe looked like a model student. He wrote home to say that as long as "I don't get frightened" he would surely succeed. In the beginning, Poe excelled because of his sharp intellect and keen memory and not because of his study habits. He could usually just spend a few minutes with the material before class and perform perfectly during an exam. Even so, he flourished. He finished assignments that other students didn't bother with - once translating an Italian Renaissance poet into English verse - and was examined at length by two former presidents of the United States, James Madison and James Monroe. He also received high honors in both ancient and modern languages.

Poe's classmates offered conflicting accounts of his time at the university. Some said that he was given to periods of melancholy, while others described manic fits of "nervous excitability." He was often a flamboyant figure, favoring his friends with bits of poetry and covering the walls of his room with charcoal sketches of "whimsical, fanciful, and grotesque figures." Once, he invited a group of students to hear a story that he'd written. He paced back and forth in front of a fireplace as he read aloud, but when one of them ventured a word of criticism, he turned and flung the entire stack of pages into the fire.

Poe spent his time in Charlottesville often desperate for money. He wrote letters home asking for books, soap, clothing, and other basics. By accident or by design, Allan had sent Poe off to school with very few funds. This was a dramatic change from Poe's early days in the Allan home, when his foster father had spared no expense to provide for him. Now, when Allan was one of the richest men in Virginia, he kept a tight hold on the purse strings and placed Poe in a situation that would soon ruin him.

After just a few weeks, Poe found himself unable to pay for his room and board. Four years later, in a bitter letter that he wrote to Allan, he still vividly recalled those days: "I will boldly say that it was wholly and entirely your own mistaken parsimony that caused all the difficulties in which I was involved at Charlottesville. The expenses of the institution at the lowest estimate were $350 annum. You sent me there with $110. I had, of course, the mortification of running in debt and was immediately regarded in the light of a beggar. You will remember that in a week after my arrival, I wrote to you for some more money and for books. You replied in the terms of utmost abuse. If I had been the vilest wretch on earth you could not have been more abusive."

Allan had hoped that a tight budget would teach Poe the skills of self-reliance. Instead, the "mortification" that Poe faced brought out the young man's worst nature. He turned to gambling to make up the shortfall, which only caused him to sink further into debt. As his losses piled up, he turned to alcohol for consolation. A friend later recalled, "Poe's passion for string drink was as marked and peculiar as that for cards. It was not the taste of the beverage that influenced him; without a sip of smack of the mouth he would seize a full glass, without water or sugar, and send it home with a single gulp."

Stories circulated about Poe's drinking problem. There were numerous reports of his wild binges and of him being found in a drunken stupor in taverns and in ditches. It didn't seem to be that Poe drank too much, but that he had a bizarre reaction to even a small amount of alcohol.

It should come as no surprise that Poe soon found that liquor and gambling are a poor mix. He racked up staggering losses - perhaps as much as $2,000, which is more than $52,000 today - or more than five times his annual expenses. He asked John Allan for money, but he refused to give it to him. In December, after only 10 months for Poe at the university, Allan came to Charlottesville, paid off a few of the debts that he considered legitimate, and removed his foster son from school.

Poe was taken back to Richmond, but his many debts followed him. Each day brought new demands for payment and new threats of legal action. Allan punished him by forcing Poe to work without pay in his firm's counting house.

Adding to Poe's distress, he also had to contend with his failed courtship of Elmira Royster, the beautiful young woman to whom he'd been secretly engaged. Poe had written to her many times from Charlottesville but had never received a letter in reply. Years later, he would find out why - her father had intercepted the letters and destroyed them. Elmira assumed that he had forgotten about her after going away to college.

After returning to Richmond, Poe attended a party at her home in hope of a reunion, only to discover that it was a celebration of her engagement to another man. Elmira was married two years later, which inspired Poe to write a poem called "Song," in which he suggested that the bride's feelings for him never faded.

After two months working in Allan's counting house, Poe's resentment boiled over into confrontation. After a bitter argument, Allan threw Poe out of the house. He found a room in a local tavern, where he sent off a letter that he spent little time thinking about before he sent it. He blasted Allan for destroying his hopes for an education and for taking delight in his failure. He demanded that his clothing and books be sent to him immediately, along with enough money to get him safely out of town. He added darkly, "If you fail to comply with my request, I tremble for the consequence."

Allan responded with his own angry letter, listing what he considered his foster son's many sins and ridiculing him for asking for more money.

When it became clear that Allan's home was truly closed to him, Poe wandered the streets of Richmond. He was penniless, starving, and desperate. Accounts vary as to what happened next, mostly depending on the romantic soul - or lack of one - of the teller. One account claims he ran into an old friend who gave him enough money to get onto a ship bound for England. Another story states that he left for Greece, to fight for the country's independence, while another claims he ended up in Russia. Allan himself confessed his uncertainty - and his indifference - in a letter he wrote to his sister.

"I'm thinking Edgar has gone to sea to seek his own fortunes," he wrote.

The truth wasn't nearly as exciting. Unable to pay for food or shelter, Poe talked himself onto a coal vessel that was sailing for Boston. He probably worked in exchange for passage. Boston was then America's literary center. Poe had a collection of poems with him as he went north. Allan had scorned his literary aspirations and Poe was determined to prove him wrong.

And there was one other reason for going to Boston, too. One of the few keepsakes left to him by his mother was a sketch of Boston Harbor with a note on the back. It read, "For my little son, Edgar, who should ever love Boston, the place of his birth, and where his mother found her best, and most sympathetic, friends."

But Poe found no sympathetic friends in Boston. He arrived there in April 1827 and served briefly as both an office clerk and a reporter. He did poorly at both and was kicked out of the boarding house where he was living after failing to pay rent.

At loose ends, Poe decided to join the army. He enlisted for a five-year stint, giving his name as "Edgar A. Perry," and listing his age as 22. He was 18 at the time.

It's impossible to know why Poe would have joined the army, although sheer desperation was likely part of it. At the very least, the military offered him three meals a day and a place to sleep. He might have also wanted to prove to John Allan that he would go to any length to make something of himself. In any event, it marked a drastic change in his life. While attending college, he had gambled away thousand of dollars. In the army, his salary was just $5 a month.

"Private Perry" spent the next six months with Battery H of the First Artillery, stationed at Fort Independence in Boston Harbor. He adapted quickly to military life, serving as a company clerk, commissary worker, and messenger. He was, needless to say, overqualified for his position in the military of the 1820s. It's fair to say there were no other army recruits who could translate Homer and Cicero and definitely no others who had published a collection of poems.

Fort Independence on Castle Island in Boston Harbor. It was Poe's first dreary military posting - it would not be his last.

In the summer of 1827, just two months after joining the army, Poe had published a 40-page booklet called *Tamerlane and Other Poems*. He had arranged for the publication before his enlistment, somehow paying for the private printing with the funds he'd collected from his various jobs. The book was credited only to "A Bostonian." The writings drew heavily on his thwarted romance with Sarah Royster with many of the poems dealing with lost love and the follies of youth. In the brief preface was a note that stated that many of the verses had been composed "when the author had not completed his fourteenth year." If by chance the book was not successful, Poe assured the readers that "failure will not at all influence him in a resolution already adopted" to succeed as a poet.

And that turned out to be a good thing.

Poe's limited resources had only allowed 50 copies of the book to be printed. This was far too few to attract serious attention from critics or readers. In fact, it got almost no attention at all.

Meanwhile, "Perry" was still doing well in the army. After six months at Fort Independence, his battery was shipped out to South Carolina in November 1827. Poe would spend more than a year at Fort Moultrie on Sullivan's Island in Charleston Harbor. In December 1828, he was moved to Fort Monroe near Hampton, Virginia, where he was given a promotion, a new job preparing artillery shells, and a raise in pay to $10 a month. He was also given a ration of liquor each day, which he apparently didn't touch. A commanding officer later praised him for his exemplary conduct, noting that he kept entirely "free of drinking." On January 1, 1829, Poe was promoted to the rank of sergeant major, the highest possible rank for a noncommissioned officer.

Fort Moultrie on Sullivan's Island in South Carolina, just off the coast of Charleston

By this time, though, Poe was tired of army life. He had endured a tedious stretch on Sullivan's Island, which he said offered "little else than the sea sand," and even the move to Fort Monroe and his promotion did little to encourage him. With three years left on his enlistment, he knew he'd reached a dead end. He confided his feelings to a sympathetic officer named Howard and revealed not only the unhappy circumstances that had led to his enlistment, but also his true age. Howard told him that a discharge might be possible but there was a condition - Poe would have to reconcile with John Allan because his permission would be required.

Begging for his foster father's help was so distasteful to Poe that it was Lieutenant Howard who ended up writing to Allan. Unfortunately, though, Poe's absence had not made Allan's heart grow fonder. He coldly informed Howard that Poe "had better remain as he is until the termination of his enlistment."

Poe's heart sank. He wanted to escape from the drudgery of the army, so he forced himself to contact Allan directly. He tried, over the course of several letters, to make the case for leaving the army and returning home. "I am altered from what you knew me and am no longer a boy tossing about on the world without aim or consistency." But, once again, Poe resorted to a subtle threat to get his point across. He wrote that he would be "driven to more decided measures if you refuse to assist me."

When the letters went unanswered, Poe altered his plan. Instead of leaving the army, he now sought help from Allan in advancing further in the ranks. Acting on the advice of Howard and several others, he asked Allan's help in securing a place at the United States Military Academy at West Point. Having already completed artillery training and proving himself to be a capable soldier, Poe expected to complete his cadet training in about six months. But, once again, he couldn't help himself, and included another veiled threat of "exile forever to another."

The only kind notes in his letters to Richmond were his consistent and genuine concern for his foster mother, Frances. He always included things like, "My dearest love to Ma - it is only when absent that we can tell the true value of such a friend - I hope she will not let my wayward disposition wear away the love she used to have for me."

Mrs. Allan's health had always been fragile but by then, she had gone into a slow and painful decline. In March 1829, Poe received the unhappy news that she had died at the age of only 44. In her final illness, she had repeatedly expressed her desire for a reunion with her foster son.

Poe took leave from the army and traveled to Richmond, where a grieving John Allan welcomed him and even bought him a new mourning suit. By the time Poe returned to his post, Allan had given consent to his plan to enter West Point. On his discharge forms from the regular army, Poe declared himself to be Allan's "son and heir."

All that remained was to finalize the discharge, which Poe botched. Regulations required him to arrange a substitute to serve the remaining years of his enlistment. Although the standard pay for this service was only $12, Poe would have to remain until his superiors returned from furlough to secure a man at this price. Unwilling to wait, he impatiently offered $75 to an ex-soldier to take his place right away. The man was given $25 in cash and a promissory note for the difference. Just like when he had left the University of Virginia two years earlier, Poe left the army with a debt that he had no way of honoring. When John Allan learned of this, the truce between the two men began to unravel.

Poe had to wait 14 months before a place opened at West Point and Allan made it clear that Poe was not welcome to wait in Richmond. He even wrote, "I am not particularly anxious to see you."

Poe traveled to Baltimore, where he lived with a cousin. He spent most of his time assembling his West Point application materials and letters of recommendation. He even managed to get one from John H. Eaton, the current Secretary of War, but had to walk 37 miles to Washington to obtain it.

He also passed the time writing for a second collection of poetry and managed to get a few of them placed in literary journals. Those poems earned a little back-handed praise, "though nonsense, rather exquisite nonsense." In May 1829, he wrote to John Allan with "a request different from any I have ever yet made," asking him for $100 to protect a publisher against loss if they agreed to publish his new book of poems. In this way, Poe believed, he could "cut out a path to reputation" without derailing his plan to enter West Point.

The request was not out of the ordinary - guarantees like this were common at the time - but Allan, who had dismissed Poe's studies of literature at the University of Virginia, was definitely not a patron of the arts. Allan not only refused the money, but he wrote to Poe and strongly criticized his plan. Undeterred, Poe took the manuscript to a small firm in Baltimore that didn't require a guarantee. The 72-page book, called *Al Aaraaff, Tamerlane, and Minor Poems*, was printed at the end of 1829. There were 250 copies printed and this time, he published it under his own name.

This new collection fared slightly better than Poe's first effort, even managing to get a handful or reviews. He was now, he said, "irrecoverably a poet." But, by this time, his application to West Point had advanced through the bureaucracy and, as he'd promised Allan, he would not let the demands of poetry divert him.

In June 1830, Poe traveled to New York to enter the United States Military Academy. It should be no surprise that he was ill suited to the rigors and harsh discipline of West Point. In those days, regulations forbid cadets to "read novels, romances, or plays,"

The United States Military Academy at West Point. When Poe tired of being a soldier, he seized on the plan to become an officer instead. But when his father disowned him, he quickly ran out of money and was unable to stay.

making it clear that the academy was not the place for an artistic temperament. He was trying to get back into his foster father's good graces, though, so he had few options.

When he arrived, Poe was immediately thrown into the difficult period of the summer encampment - sleeping rough in crude tents and undergoing endless rounds of drills and weapons training, beginning at 5:30 a.m. each day. When the academic year began in September, Poe and his fellow cadets moved into the barracks and divided their time between class work and military exercises until 10:00 p.m. Poe excelled at the academic work, but after the comparatively light duties of his army service, he considered the training and exercise to be intolerable. And he was not alone in this opinion. The size of his class dwindled from 130 cadets at the start to just 87 after less than six months.

It wasn't long before Poe also began to lose interest in his studies and began seeking refuge in a nearby tavern, whose proprietor he would recall as the "sole congenial soul in the entire god-forsaken place."

Poe had expected to breeze through his training in a mere six months but now learned that, like all the other cadets, he would be required to spend a full four years at West Point before he received a commission. It three more years in the army had seemed intolerable to Poe, then four years at West Point was undoubtedly his worst nightmare.

Meanwhile, Poe's truce with John Allan had further frayed. Although Allan had permitted a brief visit to Richmond after Poe's position at West Point was secured, the visit had gone badly, and old tensions had been revived. Allan, though, had other demands for his attention. Barely a year after Frances' death, Allan made plans to marry Louisa Patterson, a woman 20 years younger, with whom he would go on to have three children. Almost at the same time, a long-time mistress of Allan's gave birth to twin sons. For Poe, toiling away at West Point, the implications of this were obvious - he was now in a very crowded field of Allan's "sons and heirs."

Apparently, Allan was eager to get on with his life and consign Poe to a place among his late wife's discarded belongings. By the end of the year, he had engineered a division with his foster son over the money that Poe had given to his substitute when leaving the army. The man had sent several letters to Poe attempting to collect the money that was owed to him. Poe tried to explain why he couldn't pay him and, in a letter, blamed it on Allan. He claimed that Allan always "shuffled off" his requests for help, and was "not very often sober, which accounts for it." Somehow, these remarks made their way back to Allan, who sent Poe a furious letter in which he stated he would have "no further communication with yourself."

It had taken years, but John Allan had finally disowned him. Poe fired off a blistering four-page response, making a list of complaints and accusations that dated back to childhood. He demanded, "Did I, when an infant, solicit your charity and protection, or was it of your own free will that you volunteered your services on my behalf?"

He concluded the letter on a typically dramatic and self-destructive note: "You sent me to West Point like a beggar. The same difficulties are threatening me as before at Charlottesville - and I must resign."

Although Poe was unhappy about spending four years at West Point, it's likely that he saw his resignation as a way to punish Allan. Unfortunately, in order for him to withdraw, he had to have Allan's signature. Poe warned him that if he failed to honor "this last request" he would get himself kicked out of the academy and sully John Allan's reputation by doing so. Poe had already managed to rack up an impressive number of bad conduct points by this time - so, what were a few more? Allan failed to respond so Poe began a campaign of negligence, failing to report for duty on several occasions, and missing classes. Finally, on January 28, 1831, Poe was charged with neglect and disobedience. He offered no defense, which guaranteed that he would be dismissed. He wrote to Allan again, "I have been dismissed, when a single line from you would have saved it."

Surprisingly, Poe's former West Point classmates offered him the aid that John Allan had refused. In his early days at the academy, Poe had established himself as a satirist, poking fun at West Point commanders and traditions in verse. His efforts made quite an impression and after his departure, more than 100 of his classmates contributed to a fund to underwrite his third collection of poems. They raised more than $150 on his behalf and 500 copies of the resulting volume, *Poems,* came out in May 1831.

Although it featured a grateful dedication to the "United States Corps of Cadets," the book was met with disappointment in the barracks because it didn't contain any of Poe's military spoofs. One cadet wrote, "This book is a damn cheat."

Luckily for Poe, that opinion was in the minority. It turned out to be fairly well received and the 22-year-old managed to present the themes that would dominate his life and career, giving voice to a sense of loss and wretchedness that would echo in every poem and story he would ever write.

2. Horror in Print

BELIEVE NOTHING YOU HEAR, AND ONLY ONE HALF THAT YOU SEE.
— EDGAR ALLAN POE

Poe's third collection of poems may have been better received, but it failed to earn him the reputation that he'd hoped it would. In the aftermath of the break with John Allan, Poe ended up in Baltimore, where he sought out his aunt, Maria Clemm, one of the few remaining links he had to the family of his father, David Poe.

Maria's husband, William Clemm, had once been prominent in the Baltimore business community but his death five years earlier had left the family in dire financial circumstances. Maria had been reduced to taking in sewing and boarders to make ends meet.

Maria was a sweet-natured woman who bore her hardships with "martyr-like fortitude," Poe once wrote. In addition to caring for her bedridden mother, Elizabeth, she also cared for her two children, Henry, 13, and nine-year-old Virginia, as well as a steady stream of down-on-their-luck relatives, like Poe, who drifted into town. Maria welcomed Poe with open arms and after the

Poe's beloved aunt, Maria Clemm. She would be his unquestioning supporter during his entire life - and beyond.

unhappiness of Richmond, he formed an intense attachment to his aunt and would later describe her as "dearer than the mother I knew."

Hopeful about helping out his new family, Poe tried his hand at writing short stories, inspired initially by a $100 prize offered by a Philadelphia newspaper contest. Poe didn't win but he did impress the editors. Five of his stories would appear in the newspaper in 1832, including "Metzengerstein," about an orphan who exacts supernatural vengeance on those who wronged him.

Poe had turned to writing short stories out of necessity - he would always consider himself a poet first - but he had an uncanny storytelling ability.

While he worked, Maria Clemm took it upon herself to act as an intermediary between Poe and local publishers. She knew that, after being raised in wealth and extravagance, he knew little about handling money. He desperately would not allow himself to be discouraged. The following year, when Baltimore's *Sunday Visitor* offered a $50 award for the best prose tale submitted, he fired off six different submissions, finally nabbing the prize with the now famous story "MS. Found in a Bottle," a haunting story of a ghost ship and its spectral crew who find themselves at the edge of a terrifying abyss. The prospect of the unknown realm both horrifies and excites the anonymous narrator - "It is evident that we are hurrying onward to some exciting knowledge, some never-to-be-imparted secret, whose attainment is destruction."

Poe was grateful and relieved to win the prize but also felt the sting of injustice when he didn't win the $25 prize for poetry, too. He was enraged when he discovered that prize had been won by one of the paper's editors, writing under a pseudonym and the two men actually came to blows in the street. He was only 23, but Poe had already cultivated what would be a lifelong habit of fighting with editors. He just didn't ordinarily do so with his fists.

The cramped house in Baltimore where Poe lived with his aunt and cousins.

Poe and the Clemm family continued to struggle, and things became so dire that Poe was forced to swallow his pride and try to appeal to John Allan for assistance. He sent several letters in an effort to repair the division between them and declared himself "ready to curse the day I was born," when he described the conditions of abject poverty in which he lived. "I know that I have no longer any hopes of being received into your favor but, for the sake of Christ, do not let me perish for a sum of money that you would never miss," he implored his foster father.

Aware that it would be difficult for Allan to respond to Poe, Maria also wrote on his behalf, describing her nephew as a worthy soul who had fallen into temporary difficulty. Eventually, Allan relented, asking a Baltimore friend to inquire about Poe's debts and offered $20 to "keep him out of further difficulties."

In February 1834, Poe learned that Allan was seriously ill. Fearing the worst, he hurried to Richmond in hopes of a reconciliation. Allan's wife, Louisa, answered Poe's knock but did not recognize the thin, shabby figure on her doorstep. She told him that Allan was too sick to receive callers, but Poe pushed past her and burst into the sickroom. At the sight of Poe, Allan brandished his walking stick and threatened to beat him if he came any closer. The old man glared at him for a moment and then ordered him out of the house.

The rift between them would never be sealed. Allan died six weeks later, and Poe received nothing from his estate. Allan had finally made good on his threat to cast Poe out "without a shilling." He just had to die to do so. In one of his last letters to him, Poe had written, "When I think of the long twenty-one years that I have called you father, and you have called me son, I cry like a child to think it should all end in this."

Poe returned to Baltimore, where he sank deeper into poverty. He did what he could to earn money, even laboring in a brickyard for a time. When a friend, John Pendleton Kennedy, invited him to dinner one evening, Poe had to decline, humiliated that his best clothes were too threadbare for formal wear. Kennedy was resolved to lend assistance to him and recommended Poe as "very clever with a pen" to Thomas Willis White, the publisher of the *Southern Literary Messenger* in Richmond. In time, White offered Poe an editorial position at a salary of $15 per week with a chance for advancement.

Although desperate, Poe had mixed feelings about leaving Maria Clemm's home in Baltimore for Richmond, which had many unhappy memories for him. Nevertheless, he moved to Richmond in the summer of 1835, intending to help the *Southern Literary Messenger* make good on its stated goal to "stimulate the pride and genius of the South."

He quickly made his mark, impressing White with his talent and editorial skills. During his time at the helm, Poe managed every aspect of production - dealing with printers, editing copy, soliciting submissions, and writing reviews, poetry, and editorials. He also helped to increase readership of the magazine from 500 to 3,500, a remarkable achievement for the time.

Even in the midst of this success, Poe felt an overpowering sense of loneliness at his separation from Maria Clemm and his cousin, Virginia, whom he'd hoped would join him in Richmond. When word reached him that another cousin, Neilson Poe, had offered to become Virginia's guardian, and perhaps bring Maria into his home also, Poe fell into despair. To Poe, the offer would cut him off from the only true family he'd ever known, isolating him not only from Maria but from Virginia, with whom he'd fallen in love.

Poe's cousin, Neilson Poe

It is impossible to know when Poe began to have romantic feelings for Virginia, who was only nine-years-old when he first began living with her family in Baltimore. He is thought to have looked elsewhere for companionship when he first arrived in the city, but the penniless and unemployed young man was an unlikely suitor. Although it was common in those days for close cousins to marry, Virginia was only 13 when Poe started working at the *Messenger*, and her age made her a little young, even for the conventions of that time. Neilson Poe's offer to be the girl's guardian may have been a sign of his discomfort over the suitability of Virginia and Edgar together.

Although Maria had made no decision about accepting Neilson's offer, Poe responded to the possibility as a devastating loss and betrayal. He wrote Marie and tortured - and probably drunken - letter that begged her to refuse, "Oh Aunty, Aunty, you loved me once, how can you be so cruel now? I have no desire to live and will not." He finished the letter with a direct appeal to Virginia, "My love, my own sweetest sissy, think well before you break the heart of your cousin."

With the stress of the affair weighing him down, Poe turned to alcohol - a lot of it. This caused great concern for Thomas White, who had founded his magazine on principles of moral rectitude and temperance. White was fond of Poe and tried to show him compassion, assigning him to lighter duties in hopes that he would recover his "more amiable" nature. When that didn't work, he was forced to fire him. Even then, he still worried about Poe's mental state. He admitted, "I should not be at all astonished to hear that he had been guilty of suicide."

Desperate, Poe returned to Baltimore in September 1835 and managed to convince the Clemms to reject what would have been comfort and safety with Neilson Poe in favor of an uncertain future with him. It's said that Poe even went as far as to obtain a marriage license at the Baltimore County courthouse to make his offer more appealing.

The following month, Poe brought Virginia and Maria to Richmond. His departure had left the *Messenger* short-staffed so Thomas White agreed to give him a second chance - but only if Poe stopped drinking. Determined to make things work, he threw himself into editing and reviewing. By the end of December, White had given him more responsibility and noted with satisfaction that Poe had not returned to the bottle.

His editorial work at the journal was heavy and while Poe reprinted some of his earlier stories, he had little time to write new ones. One of the few original efforts that he penned during this period, though, was based on a true crime.

The Beauchamp-Sharp Murder Case - more famously known as "The Kentucky Tragedy" - involved the murder of Kentucky legislator Solomon P. Sharp. A young woman named Anna Cooke was seduced and cast aside by Sharp after she became pregnant with his illegitimate child. The child - which Sharp denied was his - was stillborn, making the situation even messier. A short time later, a young attorney named Jeroboam O. Beauchamp began courting Anna, but she only agreed to marry him on the condition that he kill Sharp and avenge her honor. Beauchamp and Cooke married in June 1824, and in the early morning of November 7, 1825, Beauchamp murdered Sharp at Sharp's home in Frankfort.

Beauchamp was quickly revealed as the killer and he was arrested at his home in Glasgow, just four days after the murder.

He was tried, convicted, and sentenced to death by hanging. He was granted a stay of execution to allow him to write a justification of his actions.

Anna was also arrested and tried for complicity in the murder, but she was acquitted due to a lack of evidence. She was utterly devoted to her husband, though, and sympathetic officials allowed her to stay in his cell with him. This led to two attempts at double suicide, once by drug overdose and the second time using a knife that Anna had smuggled into the jail. When the guards discovered them, Beauchamp was rushed to the gallows so that he could be hanged before he bled to death.

Anna died a few minutes later. According to the couple's wishes, they were positioned in an embrace and buried in the same coffin together.

The drama inspired works by some of Poe's contemporaries and a century later, it inspired *World Enough and Time* by Robert Penn Warren. With a Southern setting and a tragic young heroine, the case made an ideal subject for Poe but oddly, he decided to translate it into an Italian-themed story that was set in sixteenth century Rome. Even Poe's admirers were baffled by his choice. Early portions of the story appeared in the *Messenger* and were unanimously criticized. Poe wisely ended up leaving the story unfinished.

But he fared much better with the literary criticism that he wrote for the *Messenger* -- even though Poe would eventually use his platform to sabotage his own success.

In addition to all his other duties, he wrote nearly 100 critical pieces over a period of about 10 months. One of his more fiery reviews was about a novel by Theodore Fay called *Norman Leslie*, a forgotten book that was inspired by a New York murder case. Poe dismissed it as "the most inestimable piece of balderdash with which the common sense of the good people of America was ever so openly or so villainously insulted." Actually, though, the good people of America had liked the book and turned it into a bestseller after earning some particularly wild praise from the *New York Mirror*. Poe wasted no time in pointing out that Theodore Fay was one of the editors of the *Mirror* and accused them of a phony review. As it

Poe's wife - and cousin - Virginia. The two were married when she was only 13. She went on to die an early and tragic death.

happened, Poe's ferocious attack on the book only rallied the literary establishment to Fay's side. They would eventually turn on Poe.

In May 1836, after several months in Richmond, Poe and Virginia Clemm were married in a small ceremony. A witness attested to the fact that the young bride was 21, though in fact she was not quite 14. By all accounts, Virginia had a lovely face, dark brown hair, and violet eyes. Friends often spoke of her gentleness, kindness, and uncanny ability to bring out the best qualities in her moody husband.

Constantly reminding himself about what his new wife had given up so she could be with him, he made every effort to keep her happy. A friend later recalled that he "devoted a large part of his salary to Virginia's education, and she was instructed in every elegant accomplishment at his expense. He himself became her tutor at another time when his income was not sufficient to provide for a more regular course of instruction. I remember finding him once engaged, on a certain Sunday, in giving Virginia lessons in Algebra." On rare occasions when he had the money, he made sure that she had a piano and a harp to play.

But despite Virginia's accomplishments and Poe's attempts to give her a wonderful life, there was still the very uncomfortable situation of her age. Poe is reported to have felt considerable unease about it, but the fact that he married her at 13 is still unsettling.

There is some evidence to say that he did not "assume the position of a husband" until she turned 16, but no one can say for sure.

Not surprisingly, Poe's unorthodox marriage did seep into his work. In "Eleonora," the most romantic story he ever wrote, the narrator speaks of his obsession with the beauty of "the sole daughter of the only sister of my mother long departed," with whom he lived innocently for many years until, one fateful evening "at the close of the third lustrum of her life," they fell into one another's arms. When they were married, Virginia was far short of completing the "third lustrum of her life" - five years - but perhaps that was Poe assuring his readers that he didn't sleep with Virginia until she was of age in the 1830s.

Regardless, the marriage was an odd one by anyone's standards. Even if we leave aside the age difference between them, Virginia read little of Poe's work and he never wrote a poem about her until after she died. He was devoted to her, however, and despite his often gloomy personality and frequent odd behavior, he probably loved her very much.

Maria Clemm continued to live with the couple after they were married. Whatever may have attracted Poe to his cousin, he was appreciative of the fact that his marriage had also forged a deeper bond between himself and Maria. He declared that he was confident about a bright future when he wrote, "My health is better than for years past, my mind is fully occupied, my pecuniary difficulties have vanished, I have a fair prospect of future success - in a word, all is right."

But things wouldn't stay that way for long.

Poe may have been happy at home, but feelings of resentment had started to grow toward the *Messenger* and Thomas White. Although Poe's efforts had helped to increase the readership of the magazine many times over, and brought in an excess of $10,000, Poe continued to be paid what he called a "contemptible" salary. He would later complain that "my best energies were wasted in the service of an illiterate and vulgar, although well-meaning man, who had neither the capacity to appreciate my labors, nor the will to reward them."

So, what could Poe do that would most likely sabotage his relationship with White? He turned back to alcohol, which also meant drinking on the job. A clerk at the magazine once stated, "Mr. Poe was a fine gentleman when he was sober but when he was drinking, he was about one of the most disagreeable men I have ever met."

In January 1837, Poe was fired again. Thomas White declared, "I am as sick of his writings as I am of him."

No matter what he was being paid, Poe's failure at the *Southern Literary Messenger* was largely his own doing, setting the stage for a pattern that he would repeat again and again throughout his career. As his literary skills became more polished, so too did his genius for self-destruction, with the result that nearly every success was diminished by an alcoholic binger or other reckless behavior. His resentment grew when he found himself "debased and degraded" by having to ask White for more money, as he had often had to do with John Allan. He knew that White had profited handsomely from Poe's work so it galled him that he could barely afford to feed himself and his family.

John Allan had once sarcastically told him, "Men of genius ought not apply for my aid." Allan meant it as an insult, but it stuck with Poe. He believed he had a talent that should have been respected so much that he never should have to ask anyone to appreciate it.

With nothing to keep him in Richmond - a town that he still had bad feelings about - Poe packed up his household and moved to New York in February 1837. He believed he could find a bright new start there.

But Poe couldn't have been more wrong.

The family arrived in New York at the start of the great banking panic of 1837 and this development caused Poe to sink to new extremes of desperation. With New York and most of the rest of the country entering into a six-year economic depression, Poe found that opportunities - literary and otherwise - were in short supply.

Friends who visited their lodgings recalled an atmosphere of "threadbare gentility." The same could be said for Poe himself. He wandered the streets in a worn black suit that Virginia and Maria kept carefully brushed but there were few doors open to him. A friend observed that Poe "carried himself erect and well, as one who had been trained to it. Coat, hat, boots, and gloves had very evidently seen their best days, but so far as brushing and mending go, everything had been done, apparently, to make them presentable. On most men his clothes would have looked shabby and seedy, but there was something about this man that prevented one from criticizing his garments."

Poe brought his family to New York in 1837, just in time for a banking collapse that put him deeper into poverty.

Poe spent as much time as possible at his writing table. For months, he had been trying to find a publisher for a collection of stories that he called *Tales of the Folio Club*. The firm of Harper & Brothers seriously considered the volume but then rejected it, sending along a word of advice: "I think it would be worth your while, if other engagements permit, to undertake a Tale in a couple of volumes, for that is the magical number."

Poe took the message to heart and immediately set aside his short stories to work on a novel, *The Narrative of Arthur Gordon Pym,* which he hoped would be published in the popular two-volume format of the day. Drawing on Daniel Defoe, Jonathan Swift, and his own "MS. Found in a Bottle," he created a first-person account of a perilous sea voyage to the South Pole. Poe had featured a little of this story in the *Southern Literary Messenger* but had set it aside when his relationship with White fell apart. Now, he expanded the story and increased his output when Harper & Brothers agreed to publish it on terms they called "liberal and satisfactory."

Poe envisioned the story as an epic, as evidenced by a sprawling subtitle of more than 100 words:

Comprising the Details of Mutiny and Atrocious Butchery on Board the American Brig Grampus, on Her Way to the South Seas, in the Month of June 1827. With an Account of the Recapture of the Vessel by the Survivors; Their Shipwreck and Subsequent Horrible Sufferings from Famine; Their Deliverance by Means of the British Schooner Jane Guy; the Brief Cruise of this Latter Vessel in the Atlantic Ocean; Her Capture, and the Massacre of Her Crew Among a Group of Islands in the Eighty-Fourth Parallel of Southern Latitude; Together with the Incredible Adventures and Discoveries Still Farther South to Which That Distressing Calamity Gave Rise.

Poe loved the idea of using the story to obscure the line between fact and fiction and making the novel appear to be a true story. He even withheld his name from the title page and presented it as the work of "A.G. Pym." In the preface, "Mr. Poe" was identified as one of a group of gentlemen from Virginia who had expressed an interest in the tale. Pym explained that Poe's earlier account of the adventure - published in the *Messenger* - had been written "under the garb of fiction" from an early account of the narrative. Poe added to the illusion by including diary excerpts, logbook entries, and even portions written in hieroglyphics. At a time when little was known about Antarctica, many readers and reviewers accepted the fanciful narrative as fact. In a few places, parts of the novel were presented as "breaking news," as if Pym were a genuine explorer sending back dispatches from the icy wastes of the South Pole.

Reviews were mixed when the novel came out in July 1837, in part because the literary elite of New York and Boston had not forgotten the scathing reviews that Poe had published from Richmond. His career had barely started, and he had already hurt his reputation with powerful literary figures like Theodore Fay, whose book Poe had recently lambasted. Lewis Gaylord Clark, a supporter of Fay's, attacked the novel for its "loose and slipshod style, seldom checkered by any of the more common graces of composition."

The critics were ambivalent, but Poe still hoped that Harpers would consider publishing a collection of his short stories.

Poe was billed as the author of *The Conchologist's First Book*, a student's version of Thomas Wyatt's pricey picture book from Harpers. Poe had been paid by the author for the job, but it was seen by those who weren't aware of the situation as shameless theft - an accusation that haunted Poe for years.

But that didn't work out either - Poe managed to squander whatever goodwill he had with them with an ill-considered bit of hack work.

Harpers had recently published an expensive and lavishly-illustrated book on sea creatures called *The Manual of Conchology*, priced out of the range of most common people at $8. The author, Thomas Wyatt, had plans to put together an abridged version of the book at a lower price, in hopes that it might be sold to schools. When Harper objected, not wanting to undermine the sale of the deluxe edition, Wyatt decided that he would publish the abridged version anyway, using the name of "some irresponsible person whom it would be idle to sue for damages." In other words, a writer that was so broke that the publishing company wouldn't bother to sue because they knew it would be pointless.

And Wyatt found one - Edgar Allan Poe.

Poe assisted him in editing the book and contributed a preface and introduction to it. Although he hadn't put his name on the title page of what would be his only full-length novel - *The Narrative of Arthur Gordon Pym* - he jumped at the chance to be billed as the author for *The Conchologist's First Book: Or a System of Testaceous Malacology.* The book sold well but Poe didn't get any of the royalties. He had been so eager for the work that he agreed to a flat writing fee of $50 - a mistake that most writers have made, by the way. He also earned the dislike of Harpers for the rest of his career. They never forgave him, and charges of plagiarism and copyright infringement followed him for years to come, even though the book had been written with Wyatt's approval and support.

This marked the low point of Poe's life and he sank even deeper into what he called "a state of pecuniary embarrassment." Soon he declared himself willing to accept any kind of work, no matter how menial, so he could lift himself from the "literary drudgery" in which he felt he was trapped. He was very aware that he had "no other capital" except for "whatever reputation I may have acquired as a literary man," but he had managed to squander even that.

After a few months in New York, Poe was unable to get work of any kind. He decided to try his luck elsewhere. In the early months of 1839, Poe, Virginia, and Maria packed up and moved to Philadelphia. They settled into a small house on Sixteenth Street.

It had now been more than two years since he'd left the *Southern Literary Messenger* and he'd foundered badly since then. He was reluctant to submit himself to another magazine publisher, but he needed to work - and to get paid. With no other options, he made an overture to William Burton, the publisher of *Burton's Gentleman's Magazine,* about the possibility of an editorial position.

Poe's appeal to Burton shows how desperate he was at the time. By this time, Poe had been a rabid reader of reviews of his own work. I think it was simply because he loved to torture himself. He never forgot an insult. Perhaps the most scathing review of *The Narrative of Arthur Gordon Pym* had been written by William Burton, the man from whom he was now seeking a job. Burton had written, "A more impudent attempt at humbugging the public has never been exercised. We regret to find Mr. Poe's name in connexion with such a mass of ignorance and effrontery."

To Poe's relief, Burton was in a receptive state of mind. Burton, an Englishman who had made a name for himself in

Philadelphia as a comic actor, most resembled his most popular role - Sir John Falstaff, the fun-loving buffoon friend of Prince Hal in the Shakespearean play. He was a man of extraordinary energy and wide interests and got into the magazine business with the intention of creating a journal "worthy of a place upon every parlor table of every gentleman in the United States." When Poe arrived looking for work, only a few hundred gentlemen had bothered to clear a spot on the parlor table for the publication, and the publisher,

William Burton, the publisher of *Burton's Gentleman's Magazine*

who divided his time between editing and acting, needed help.

In June, Poe's name appeared next to Burton's as the magazine's assistant editor. It was an impressive title, but the salary wasn't. Claiming heavy expenses, Burton told Poe that he could only pay him $10 per week, promising a raise if things worked out. Burton told him that his responsibilities would be light, requiring no more than two hours each day, which would allow Poe to write in his spare time. Poe was in no position to bargain and he accepted the salary, which, while meager, was better than what he had been bringing in.

Initially, Poe did most of the same things he had done at the *Messenger*. He contributed filler pieces to the magazine while performing basic proofreading and other chores. Poe also resumed the savage criticism of his days at the *Messenger* and weighed in on topics that ranged from mundane housekeeping tips to offering romantic advice.

He also began hammering out new short stories of his own. In "The Man That Was Used Up," a military officer whose commanding figure has been whittled away by numerous battle wounds is reassembled using false limbs, chest and shoulder pieces, and other mechanical prosthetics.

He failed to finish a novella called "The Journal of Julius Rodman," another imaginary travel adventure that moved the action from the South Pole to the Rocky Mountains - which seemed nearly as far away to most people at the time. Poe drew heavily on the reports of Lewis and Clark, and his fiction ended up being mistaken as fact by some, with the unexpected result that parts of the story were later incorporated into a government report about the Oregon Territory.

Then, in the September 1839 issue of *Burton's* Poe published "The Fall of the House of Usher." Seizing on the conventions of Gothic horror, he created a tale of psychological torment that would form the backbone of the rest of his career.

The story features one of Poe's unnamed narrators, who arrived at the home of his friend, Roderick Usher, after receiving a letter from him complaining of an illness and asking for help. When he arrives, the narrator notices a thin crack on the outside of the house. It extends from the roof, down the front of the house, and into the adjacent lake.

It is revealed that Roderick and his sister, Madeline, are the only remaining members of the Usher family and that Madeline is also sick, sometimes falling into cataleptic, deathlike trances.

The narrator attempts to cheer his friend by reading to him and listening to his unusual musical compositions, including the "Haunted Palace," after which Usher tells his friend that he believes the house he lives in to be alive. Further, Roderick believes that his fate is connected to the family mansion.

Things take a dire turn when Usher informs the narrator that Madeline has died. Fearing that her body will be exhumed for medical study, Roderick insists that she be entombed for two weeks in the family tomb located in the house before being permanently buried. The narrator assists Roderick as Madeline is prepared for burial and then entombed in the house.

Over the next week, both men become increasingly agitated, but when a storm begins, Roderick becomes hysterical. The narrator attempts to calm his friend by reading to him from a medieval romance about a knight who tries to take a treasure from a dragon by tearing apart the walls of the place where it hides.

At this point in the story, both men heard cracking and tearing sounds somewhere in the house. A scream reverberates at the same time the dragon screams in the story. At first, the narrator ignores the noises, but Roderick becomes increasingly upset and eventually declares that he has been hearing these sounds for days. They are sounds made by his sister, he cries, who he fears was entombed alive.

Moments later, the bedroom door is forced open to reveal Madeline, covered in blood after her escape from her tomb. In a fit of rage, she attacks her brother, scaring him to death as she herself dies. The narrator then runs from the house, and, as he does, he notices a flash of moonlight behind him. He turns back in time to see the moon shining through the suddenly widened crack in the house. As he watches, the House of Usher splits in two and it sinks into the dark waters of the lake.

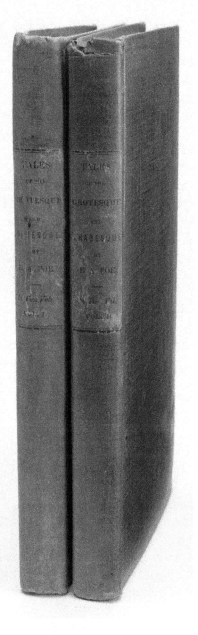

It would turn out to be one of Poe's most famous horror stories and received wide praise when it appeared. It also brought

Poe welcome attention as a writer of serious fiction. Thanks to this, he was offered a contract with the Philadelphia publishing house Lea & Blanchard to put out *Tales of the Grotesque and Arabesque* in December 1839. It was to be a two-volume collection of all of Poe's short stories to date, many of them revised for its publication. But in spite of the success of "The Fall of the House of Usher," the publisher had little confidence in the book and offered him no advance and no royalties. Instead, Poe was offered 20 free copies.

Poe wrote a letter to author Washington Irving and asked him to endorse the book, writing, "If I could be permitted to add even a word or two from yourself... my fortune would be made."

Aside from a few of the stories, the two books did not contain any of Poe's best-known works. Among the stories were "Morella," Ligeia," "King Pest," "Berenice" and some of his recent stories like "MS. Found in a Bottle," and, of course, "The Fall of the House of Usher." Reviews were mixed with some praising the collection's "opulence of imagination" while others complained that it lacked "anything of elevated fancy or fine humor." The book sold poorly and when Poe suggested a revised edition, the publisher declined, claiming that sales had not even covered the printing bill.

It is likely not a surprise to learn that by this time, Poe was becoming disenchanted with William Burton and his magazine. Thomas White had deferred to Poe in most matters of editorial judgment, but Burton had confidence in his own literary talents and largely regarded Poe as little more than a glorified office boy. Although the magazine had gotten a lot of attention for "The Fall of the House of Usher," as well as other contributions by Poe, Burton took issue with the other man's "morbid tone" and "jaundiced" frame of mind, which were at odds with what Burton saw as the otherwise cheery tone of the magazine. Poe, for his part, resented the fact that Burton failed to notice the work that he put into each issue and, of course, failed to pay him what he believed he was worth. Once again, Poe found himself in the embarrassing position of having to beg someone for money.

By May 1840, Burton's theatrical aspirations had led him to make plans for a national theater in Philadelphia. He was much too busy now, he decided, to divide his time between literature and the stage and so he began arranging the sale of the magazine.

However, he neglected to mention this to Poe.

The assistant editor found out when he saw a newspaper advertisement about the sale. Realizing that he might soon be out of a job, Poe scrambled to capitalize on his position before it was gone for good. He drew up plans for a new literary monthly called *The Penn Magazine*, in hopes of fulfilling a dream of being the editor of his own magazine. Poe promised that the journal would operate "without reference to particular regions" and would be free of "any tincture of the buffoonery, scurrility, or profanity" that could be found in other publications.

Burton was enraged when he learned of Poe's scheme. Realizing that Poe's departure would lower the value of *Burton's,* he fired him on the spot. Poe was so angry that he hurled abuse at Burton and stormed out of the office. Not content to leave it at that, Poe then fired off an angry letter, "Your attempts to bully me excite in my mind scarcely any other sentiment than mirth... If by accident you have taken it into your head that I am to be insulted with impunity, I can only assume you are an ass."

To his friends, Poe painted his departure from the magazine as one of principle, claiming that he couldn't tolerate Burton's underhanded editorial dealings. Burton offered his own self-serving take on the incident, complaining that Poe's drinking had caused him considerable annoyance. "I could obtain damages," he told one colleague.

Poe argued this. "I pledge you, before God, the solemn word of a gentleman, that I am temperate even to rigor - my sole drink is water." Even Poe's close friends had a hard time taking this statement seriously. There are many drunken accounts of him in Philadelphia and one friend even reported finding him once sprawled in a gutter.

Energized by his fighting with Burton, Poe doubled his efforts to launch his own magazine. In the end, though, failure was inevitable. The ongoing bank panic made it impossible for Poe to raise any money, although he would later insist that the first issue had been produced and was being readied for the printer when it all fell apart.

Meanwhile, Burton went ahead with his sale and in October 1840, the magazine was purchased by a Philadelphia attorney named George Graham. He already owned another magazine called *Casket*, which he planned to combine with *Burton's*, giving the new *Graham's Lady's and Gentleman's Magazine* a healthy subscriber list of 5,000 readers.

Magazine publisher George Graham, who was more tolerant than most when it came to Poe and his many eccentricities.

Even though Burton had warned Graham of his former assistant editor's shortcomings, Graham offered Poe a job soon after taking over the magazine. Even though he'd been looking for independence, Poe knew an opportunity when he saw it. In February 1841, he signed on as the editor with a salary of $800 a year, a good increase over what he'd been making before. Graham gave him a warm welcome in the pages of the new magazine: "Mr. Poe is too well known in the literary world to require a word of commendation." Poe was pleased by the new position and even more pleased that he was no longer expected to handle the entire load of proofreading and all the other drudgery. Graham himself solicited and chose most of the material in the magazine, a job he did with a good handle on public taste, leaving Poe free for more "elevated" contributions. It was agreed that each issue would feature an original Poe story, for which he would also receive contributor's pay on top of his salary.

Poe happily threw himself into his work and his affection for his genial, outgoing employer began to grow. At 27, Graham was four years younger than Poe, which made it easier for the two men to get along. Poe admired the young editor's willingness to spend money and to make the magazine successful. He commissioned original illustrations and passed on reprinted articles in favor of fresh material. Under Graham's lenient style, Poe began to thrive, and the magazine became an immediate success. During the first year, the circulation jumped from 5,000 to 40,000 subscribers.

Poe was successful at last, which, naturally meant that he would have to do something to ruin everything.

At first, Poe was sympathetic to the idea of Graham attracting a broader, less literary audience to the magazine. It was certainly not what Poe planned for his own magazine, but he understood it. He began a popular series of articles about cryptography, which resulted in readers sending in coded messages for him to solve. He also resumed his literary criticism. Although he claimed to have ceased the "causticity" of his younger days, his work at *Graham's* didn't seem any less mean-spirited. Other critics, he believed, were too quick to praise, with the result of every new poet or writer that came along being praised as a genius. That wouldn't do for Poe.

His feelings on this matter really boiled down to the fact that he believed his own genius had been overlooked in favor of lesser talents. Poe's critiques brought him a lot of attention - and attacks on his arrogance - but his work for *Graham's* did rise to a high standard and included several of his most exceptional short stories.

Among the stories was "A Descent into the Maelström," in which a man recounts how he survived a shipwreck and a whirlpool. It's been regarded as one of the earliest in the science fiction genre.

For those who love Poe's horror, *Graham's* was the first to publish "The Masque of the Red Death." The story takes place in the abbey of Prince Prospero, where the prince and 1,000 of his nobles have taken refuge to escape the Red Death, a terrible plague with gruesome symptoms that has swept over the land. Victims suffer from sharp pains, sudden dizziness, and profuse bleeding at the pores, and it kills them within a half hour of exposure. Prospero and his court are indifferent to the sufferings of the common people,

THE DANCER DROPPED GLEAMING UPON
THE SABLE CARPET

One of the most famous illustrations for "The Masque of the Red Death" by created by artist Harry Clarke in 1919.

planning to wait out the plague in luxury, secure behind the doors of the palace, which have been welded shut.

Prospero holds a masquerade ball one night to entertain his guests in seven colored rooms of the abbey. Each of the first six rooms is decorated and illuminated in a specific color -- blue, purple, green, orange, white, and violet. The last room is decorated in black, and the lighting is dark red - "a deep blood color." Few of the guests are brave enough to enter this final room. A large black clock is positioned there, and it ominously chimes each hour. When it does, everyone stops talking or dancing and the orchestra stops playing. When the chimes stop, everyone resumes their revelry.

But when the clock chimes at midnight, Prospero and the party-goers notice a figure in a dark, blood-splattered robe that looks like a funeral shroud. The figure's mask is the rigid face of a corpse that bears all the symptoms of the Red Death.

Insulted that someone would wear a reminder of the plague to his party, Prospero demands to know the identity of the mysterious guest. But everyone is too afraid to approach the figure as he passes through the six colored chambers. Prospero draws his own knife and goes in pursuit, finally cornering the figure in the seventh room. But when the figure turns to fall him, Prospero lets out a loud cry and falls dead to the floor. The enraged and terrified revelers rush into the black room and forcibly remove the figure's mask and robe, only to find to their horror that there is nothing underneath.

The costume only contains the Red Death itself, which is then contracted by the guests, who die from the disease. The final line of the story is a classic -- "And Darkness and Decay and the Red Death held illimitable dominion over all."

This story is a work of genius, there's no question about it. Poe invented the Red Death for the story, but it might have been inspired by tuberculosis - or consumption as it was known then - since Virginia had recently been diagnosed with the disease when the story was written. Like the character Prince Prospero, Poe tried to ignore the terminal nature of the disease - a disease that had killed his mother, his brother, William, and his foster mother, Frances Allan.

It would also be during his time at *Graham's* that he would earn the title of "the father of mystery stories," although that appreciation would come many years after his death. Readers loved Poe's first account of C. Auguste Dupin, but it would be years later before "The Murders in the Rue Morgue" was recognized as one of the greatest detective stories of all time.

Poe had been growing ever more fascinated with deductive reasoning and this story put it to good use. Blending artistic temperament with a scientific turn of mind, Poe introduced Dupin, his master detective. Born to an illustrious family, a "variety of untoward events" had reduced Dupin to being content with the basic necessities of life. Once again, Poe uses the unnamed narrator to tell the story, a young man who winds up sharing lodging with Dupin in Paris. During a stroll one evening, Dupin reveals an astonishing talent. Though the pair had been walking in silence for 15 minutes, Dupin suddenly breaks into his companion's thoughts with an offhand remark that seems to show that he can read the other man's mind. Dupin details his private thoughts as if his friend had spoken them aloud. Stunned, the narrator demands an explanation and Dupin easily reconstructs every link in his companion's train of thoughts, all based on his careful deduction of everything around them as they walked.

The narrator was amazed - as Dr. John Watson will also be decades later when he observes his friend, Sherlock Holmes, doing the same thing. There is no doubt that Poe had much to do with the creation of that character, too.

Soon after, the narrator draws Dupin's attention to an unusual item in the newspaper. A shocking outrage has occurred at a home on the miserable street known as the Rue Morgue. In the middle of the night, neighbors were roused by the sound of "terrific shrieks" coming from the fourth floor. When the police arrived, they forced their way into the room, only to find a scene of the "wildest disorder" - broken furniture, valuables strewn about, and a blood-smeared razor sitting on a hair, several clumps of gray hair, and two bags of gold coins.

The two women who own the house, Madame L'Espanaye and her daughter, have been killed and mutilated. The mother was found in a yard behind the house, with her throat so deeply cut that it nearly severed her head. The daughter was found strangled to death and stuffed upside down into a chimney. The door to the room was locked from the inside.

The police were utterly baffled and none of the detectives could come up with a motive for the crime or a method by which it was committed. There was also no clue as to how the killer got out of the room since the doors and windows were locked from the inside and the chimney was too small for man to escape through. The two women led quiet lives, had no enemies, and the murderer had left behind at least 4,000 francs in gold coins.

Matters became more confusing when they questioned the neighbors. Several witnesses reported hearing two voices at the time of the murder. One was a man, speaking French, but all disagreed on the language spoken by the other. The second voice was shrill and seemed to be in a foreign tongue, though no two neighbors could agree on a country of origin.

A bank clerk named Adolphe Le Bon, who had delivered the gold coins to the women on the previous morning, was arrested even though no evidence linked him to the crime. Remembering a service that Le Bon once performed for him, Dupin becomes intrigued and offers his assistance to the police and they allow him to investigate the crime scene.

The following day, Dupin announces that he has solved the crime. Because none of the witnesses can agree on the language spoken by the second voice, Dupin concludes they were not hearing a human voice at all. He dismisses the robbery motive - the gold was not taken - and points out that the killer would have had to have incredible strength to force the daughter's

Illustration for by "The Murders in the Rue Morgue" created by Daniel Vierge in 1870

body up the chimney. He describes how the murderer could have entered the room and killed both women, involving an agile climb up a lightning rod and a leap to a set of open window shutters. With the clump of hair recovered at the scene and demonstrating that it would have been impossible to strangle the daughter by human hand, Dupin concludes that an orangutan killed the women. He has placed an advertisement in the local newspaper asking if anyone has lost such an animal, and a sailor soon arrives looking for it.

The sailor offers to pay a reward but Dupin only wants the details of how the murders occurred. The sailor, who caught the orangutan in Borneo, brought it to Paris as a pet. At first, all was well, and the creature was docile. He even saw the orangutan attempting to shave its face with his straight razor, imitating the sailor's morning grooming. Soon, though, he lost control of the wild beast and it fled into the streets and reached the Rue Morgue, where it climbed up and into the house. The sailor chased after it but there was nothing he could do to stop it.

The orangutan entered the apartment, seized the mother by the hair and was waving the razor, imitating a barber. When the woman screamed in fear, it flew into a rage, ripped her hair out, slashed her throat, and strangled the daughter. The sailor climbed up the lightning rod to try and catch the animal, and the two "voices" heard by witnesses belonged to the sailor and the ape. Fearing punishment by its master, the orangutan threw the mother's body out the window and stuffed the daughter into the chimney before fleeing.

Once Dupin reveals all this to the police, the charges against the falsely accused bank clerk are dropped. The head of the police department is, of course, irritated at having been shown up by the detective and indulges in "a sarcasm or two about the propriety of every person minding his own business."

Dupin doesn't care. "Let him talk," he tells his friend. "I am satisfied with having defeated him in his own castle."

"The Murders in the Rue Morgue" appeared in the April 1841 issue of *Graham's* and received a great deal of notice. One critic even praised the author as a "man of genius."

Poe based the character of Dupin on Eugène-François Vidocq, a French criminal turned detective who helped to create the Sûreté, the detective bureau of the French police.

Eugène-François Vidocq, the basis for Poe's detective, Auguste Dupin

Vidocq is considered to be the father of modern criminology, introducing innovations like ballistics, footprint molds, and a criminal database to the detection of crime. At the time of Poe's writing, he was still active in Paris and also served as the inspiration for Jean Valjean in Victor Hugo's *Les Miserables*. Vidocq's memoirs, though largely fanciful, had recently been a public phenomenon and were undoubtedly read by Poe. Dupin even mentions Vidocq in the story, although believes himself to be a superior detective.

For all of Dupin's bluster, Poe had a keen sense of the limitations of the character. A handful or reviewers pointed out that there could be no great skill in presenting a solution to a mystery of the author's own creation. Poe himself was well aware of this. The effect of the story, no matter how ingenious, had much to do with the fact that it was "written backward" with the solution worked out in advance. A real-life detective like Vidocq had no solution to guide his investigations.

This problem nagged at Poe. For several years, he'd had an interest in real crimes, puzzles, and ciphers. Now, he wondered if he could take Dupin and apply the character's traits to a real mystery.

And it was at this point when Poe became embroiled in a real-life murder mystery that continues to haunt researchers and biographers of the writer to this day.

3. The Beautiful Cigar Girl

MEN HAVE CALLED ME MAD; BUT THE QUESTION IS NOT YET SETTLED, WHETHER MADNESS IS OR IS NOT THE LOFTIEST INTELLIGENCE— WHETHER MUCH THAT IS GLORIOUS— WHETHER ALL THAT IS PROFOUND— DOES NOT SPRING FROM DISEASE OF THOUGHT— FROM MOODS OF MIND EXALTED AT THE EXPENSE OF THE GENERAL INTELLECT.
— EDGAR ALLAN POE

On July 28, 1841, two New Yorkers were walking along the Hoboken shoreline near the spring at Sybil's Cave, then a popular tourist attraction, when they spotted a body floating out in the Hudson River. As they waited on shore for the coroner to arrive, a man walked up to them and claimed that he recognized the corpse from its clothing. It was, he told them, the body of Mary Cecilia Rogers - the missing woman who had recently been in the papers.

Her life story is a bit murky, but Mary Rogers was probably born in Lyme, Connecticut in 1820. She and her widowed mother,

The body of Mary Rogers, discovered in the Hudson River in 1841

Phoebe, moved to Manhattan in the 1830s. Phoebe opened a boarding house at 126 Nassau Street and Mary took a sales job at Anderson's Tobacco Emporium, which had become a fixture of New York's emerging social scene. It was especially popular with young men and local writers such as Washington Irving and James Fenimore Cooper. But while the customers came for owner John Anderson's tobacco, they stayed for Mary, who was dubbed "The Beautiful Cigar Girl" by the local press.

Within a year of starting work at the cigar shop, Mary had become a local celebrity, even sparking a short-lived panic when she failed to show up for work one day in 1838. Though it made headlines, this "disappearance" was dismissed as a publicity stunt for Anderson's store.

But was it? No one knows, but soon afterward, Mary left her position at the store and returned home to help her mother run her business. While her life was more private at the boarding house, she still managed to attract a lot of attention from men. She had a lot of admirers who stayed at - and hung around - the house but Mary gave all her attention to Daniel Payne, a cork cutter and boarder who became her fiancé in the summer of 1841.

Daniel would also become the last person to see Mary alive - other than her killer, that is.

One of the hundreds of newspaper illustrations of Mary Rogers - the "Beautiful Cigar Girl" - after her murder. The case became a sensation in New York and across the nation.

On the morning of July 25, Mary left the Rogers' boarding house, telling her mother that she planned to visit an aunt uptown. What happened after that - as the hours without word from her turned to days - remains unknown.

At first, it was suggested that she had simply run away, perhaps in another attempt to get attention. Daniel, though, worried about the gangs of robbers and rapists whose exploits were then filling the pages of the papers. After two days of searching, growing more convinced that Mary had been kidnapped, he had a "missing" notice printed.

The notice caught the eye of a man named Arthur Crommelian. He was a former boarder at her mother's house and had once courted Mary. He took his search across the ferry to Hoboken, arriving just in time to witness the recovery of Mary's body from the Hudson River and to identify the corpse. After he was questioned by the police and they were convinced that Crommelian's arrival on the scene didn't implicate him in the murder, the authorities turned their attention to other lead suspects.

One of the first people they questioned was John Anderson, Mary's employer, who had often accompanied her home in the evenings. Even though he could offer no alibi for the day of her disappearance, he was released when attention began to focus on Mary's fiancé, Daniel Payne.

Not only was he the last person to see Mary alive but there were rumors that the couple had been fighting and that Mary had threatened to call off the wedding. None of that turned out to be true and after Daniel produced a solid alibi, the case quickly went cold.

THE HOUSE WHERE MARY ROGERS WAS LAST SEEN ALIVE.

Newspaper illustration showing Nick Moore's Tavern and the "Murder Thicket."

Meanwhile, newspapers all over the country kept a running commentary about the case, especially in regard to what they claimed was the "bungling investigation" by the New York police. One report complained about the "slovenly manner in which the coroner at Hoboken performs his duties," while outside Philadelphia, other papers wondered if the death had been a suicide. Even New York Governor William H. Seward got involved, announcing in several New York papers a $750 reward for any information that helped solve the crime.

Then, in early September 1841, there seemed to be a break in the case. A group of boys were playing in a field in Weehawken, New Jersey - not far from where Mary's body had been found - and discovered bundles of bloody clothing in some bushes. After the discovery in what came to be called the "Murder Thicket," one of the boys' mothers, Frederica Loss, who operated the nearby Nick Moore House pub, contacted the police.

But Frederica Loss seemed to know a lot more about the case than just about the discovery of bloody clothes. When the police questioned her, she admitted that Mary Rogers had checked into the Nick Moore House on the night of her death with an unknown man. The pair had gone out but had never returned to the pub. Frederica said that she didn't think too much of it at the time but remembered hearing someone screaming in the woods later that night. Although it seems strange that she never shared this with the police before now, detectives were apparently satisfied with her answers.

Things took another turn less than a month later, on October 7, when Daniel Payne made a trip to the "Murder Thicket" after spending the evening drinking in Hoboken. While sitting on a nearby bench, he drank an entire bottle of laudanum and died from an overdose. His body was found only a few hundred yards from where Mary's corpse had been discovered. A note in his pocket read, "To the World–Here I am on the spot. God forgive me for my misfortune in my misspent time."

Without easy answers, the press once again created their own version of events. As a single working woman, Mary became a kind of symbol for the era's problems and a warning to parents about the fate that might befall their own daughters in the big city. Many papers even claimed - with no evidence, of course - that Mary had been a prostitute and even hinted that she deserved her fate.

The New York public might have been satisfied with such weak solutions, but in Philadelphia, Edgar Allan Poe was not. Mary's first "disappearance" had occurred while Poe was living in New York and he remembered it well. As the news of her fate reached him through newspaper reports, he became obsessed with the story and followed every detail.

Poe was now living well in Philadelphia. His annual salary of $800 from *Graham's Magazine*, although far from a fortune, afforded him a stability like none he'd ever had in his adult life. By the end of 1841, he'd moved his wife and mother-in-law into a small townhouse on Coates Street in the north end of the city. As he had promised long ago in Richmond, he was finally providing Virginia with the kind of comfort she deserved. Their new home was even furnished with a small

The townhouse on Coates Street in Philadelphia where Poe was living when he wrote his fictional story based on the Mary Rogers murder.

piano, a harp, and a pair of songbirds in a gilded cage.

On January 20, 1842, the day after Poe turned 33, a small group of friends gathered in the parlor of the townhouse to hear Virginia play the harp and sing. It was a perfect evening. Virginia was wearing a white gown and looked angelic in the fire light. As she tapped at the keys of the piano, she sang. The notes became higher, true, and clear - and then stopped. Virginia clutched at her throat and then choked out a cascade of blood, staining the front of her dress with crimson.

Poe's face went white. He carried Virginia upstairs, laid her on the bed, and then ran for a doctor. Poe must have known, even before the doctor grimly confirmed it, that the hemorrhage signaled the final stages of tuberculosis. He also must have known that her chances for survival were slim. By the time a patient begins coughing up blood, they were usually beyond help. Even if she could have been helped - perhaps by moving to a healthier climate or by a stay at a sanatorium - such things were well beyond the means of an editor making $800 a year.

Virginia spent the next two weeks scarcely able to breathe except when fanned with fresh air. At times, her coughing became so severe that it seemed as if she would choke to death. She pressed

Although it has not been confirmed or authenticated, it is believed that this is the only photograph in existence of Poe's beloved wife, Virginia.

a handkerchief to her mouth to cover it when she coughed, and it was often spattered red with blood.

Heart aching, Poe remained by her side, brooding over the poverty-stricken existence that he'd forced Virginia into as his wife that was now killing her. More than one visitor commented that the cramped house where they lived - luxurious compared to other places where they'd lived - was likely making Virginia's condition worse. Her sickroom was so small that the sloped roof was almost as low as her head.

George Graham, Poe's employer, noted that Poe's "love for his wife was a sort of rapturous worship of the spirit of beauty which he felt was fading before his eyes. I have seen him hovering around her when she was ill, with all the fond fear and tender anxiety of a mother for her first-born, her slightest cough causing him to shudder, a heart-chill that was visible."

Virginia's health seeped into Poe's work, most notably in the mentioned "The Masque of the Red Death," published just months before the January attack. He dwelt on themes of horror and blood because, even then, he knew what was coming. He'd seen it before with his mother when he was a small child.

In "Eleonora," also written in the early stages of Virginia's illness, Poe returned to the theme and delved into the grim circumstances of his new life. The story was about a young man living an idyllic life with his young cousin, Eleonora, and her mother. All too soon, though, Eleonora tells him that "she had seen that the finger of Death was upon her bosom - that, like the ephemeron, she had been made in perfect loveliness only to die."

In the months that followed, Poe wavered back and forth between optimism and utter despair. In February, he told friends that she was getting better, but by July, he declared that "I have scarcely a faint hope for her recovery."

For a time, Poe threw himself into his work, writing poems, stories, and reviews for *Graham's Magazine* and finding that his reputation was growing. When he learned that Charles Dickens would be touring Philadelphia in March 1842, he wrote to request an interview, sending along a copy of his *Tales of the Grotesque and Arabesque*. He also included

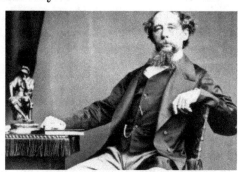

In 1842, Poe interviewed famed British novelist Charles Dickens. The novelist was impressed with the younger man and praised him for his writing and reviews.

copies of his past reviews for Dickens' work, attesting to admiration for the writer he once called "the greatest British novelist." Among them was an article he wrote about the mystery *Barnaby Rudge*, written shortly after Dickens' story began to appear in serial form. Although the book's conclusion would not be published for several months, Poe was able to predict - correctly - that "Barnaby, the idiot, is the murderer's own son."

Dickens was impressed by Poe. He gave two lengthy interviews to him at Philadelphia's United States Hotel on March 7, 1842. Dickens took particular note of Poe's reviews and would later describe him as a man "who taketh all of us English men of letters to task in print, roundly, and uncompromisingly."

Even though the interview was part of his work for *Graham's*, Poe used it to his own advantage. By the end of the meeting, Dickens had agreed to help Poe find a publisher in England. The two men parted on good terms and Dickens' work would make itself felt in Poe's own work - especially in the case of the talkative raven that appears within the pages of *Barnaby Rudge*.

Despite his position at *Graham's* being the best job that Poe had ever had, he began to fall into the same resentful state of mind that had led to difficulties at his earlier positions. No one recognized the greatness of Edgar Allan Poe like Poe himself did.

In this case, though, Poe did have some actual cause for irritation. The magazine's extraordinary success was making a fortune for Graham, but Poe's salary had stayed the same. He now considered them so pitiful that it was almost an insult. As gloom set in over Virginia's illness, his bitterness deepened. On the morning after the initial hemorrhage, Poe asked Graham to advance him two months' salary to help ease the unexpected burden. Graham refused.

At the same time, the success of *Graham's* rekindled Poe's hopes for a magazine of his own. This was another source of grievance against his employer, however. Graham had promised when Poe joined his magazine that he would help to launch Poe's own *Penn* magazine within a year. But as *Graham's* grew in circulation and became more profitable, the promise was forgotten. Poe was a victim of his own success. He later wrote, "Every exertion made by myself" served to make *Graham's* a "greater source of profit" and left its owner "less willing to keep his word with me."

The matter reached a crisis point in April 1842. After a brief time away caused by illness, Poe returned to the office to find that his duties had been taken over by Charles Peterson, an associate editor. It may be that Peterson simply covered for Poe while the other man was away, but we only know Poe's side of it, and he was offended. Always sensitive about his status as an editor, he believed that he'd been slighted and perhaps even passed over for a promotion. So, he quit.

As usual, there would be a difference of opinion as to whether Poe left or was fired. Graham later said, "Either Peterson or Poe would have to go. The two cannot get along together." Poe insisted that he left to pursue his own interests, citing his disgust with the "namby pamby" mainstream character of the magazine and the "insulting" salary. In contrast to his hostility toward Thomas White and William Burton, though, Poe spoke well of Graham and claimed to have "no misunderstanding" with him.

Whatever the reason for leaving, Poe soon found himself broke again. With Virginia's illness adding to his worries, we can only puzzle over why Poe would make such a change. We can only assume that he simply couldn't help sabotaging himself. There were very few studies of mental illness in those days and certainly, there was no one who could get inside the head of Edgar Allan Poe. He often spoke of the "nervous restlessness that haunted me as a fiend" as a reason for many of the things that he did that might seem baffling to others. He used the excuse of wanting to start a magazine of his own as a reason for leaving, but deep down, he surely knew that he would never be able to afford. He was a man of incredible talent, but he seemed eager to destroy his reputation. This marked the beginning of what some have called Poe's "irregularities," which, for the rest of his life, would destroy his hopes and put his reputation into the hands of people who hated him."

Those "irregularities" began almost at once. For the most part, Poe had stayed away from liquor during his time at *Graham's*, but now he returned to the bottle with devastating consequences. As mentioned earlier, Poe had a dramatically low tolerance for alcohol. It wasn't how much he drank; it was that he drank at all. He seemed to have a strange reaction to it. At a time when dram shops and taverns lined the streets, Poe's lack of tolerance left him uniquely vulnerable. He could never stop with a single drink. Even the first drink transformed him from a personable man to a coarse, staggering drunk. His friend Frederick Thomas noted, "if he took but one glass of weak wine or cider... it always ended in excess and sickness."

Poe's excuses for drinking were plain enough - Virginia's illness, his poverty, his literary disappointments - but turning to

After leaving - or losing - his position at Graham's, Poe began drinking heavily as a way to cope with his worries about poverty, lack of work, and Virginia's illness.

alcohol always made things worse. For instance, over the course of the 14 months that he worked at *Graham's*, he made about $1,000 in salary and contributor's fees. His literary income over the next three years added up to only $121.

All thanks to the bottle.

Poe now abandoned his writing, or at least began to supplement it with less taxing forms of work. Although he still dreamed of starting his own magazine, he also pursued the possibility of a job at the Philadelphia Customs House. It was a government job and it paid well. But Poe failed to get a local appointment, so he traveled to Washington in hopes of pleading his case directly to President Tyler, whose son Robert was a fan of Poe's writing. Nervous about the important interview, he attempted to calm his nerves with a glass of port. Soon after, he was seen stumbling around the city with a green tint to his face and his coat turned inside out. Poe did not meet the president, nor did he make a favorable impression on anyone who might have helped him to obtain the employment he was seeking.

Back at his writing desk, Poe sought new publishers for some of his magazine stories. Earlier, while working at *Graham's,* he had written to Lea & Blanchard, the publishers of *Tales of the*

Grotesque and Arabesque, to offer a revised collection of his work, expanded to include some news stories, like "The Murders in the Rue Morgue." They declined, replying that they had not yet sold out of the first edition. Despite the refusal, Poe did hope to work with them again in the future.

His hopes may have been raised further when Lea & Blanchard published a book by William Gilmore Simms called *Beauchampe,* which took inspiration from the real-life Beauchamp-Sharpe murder case in 1825. That story had also been the inspiration for an unfinished work by Poe. Believe it or not, Poe actually admired William Gilmore Simms and had once called him "immeasurably the best writer of fiction in America." So, there's no doubt that he was aware of this book and, undoubtedly, took note of the way that Simms had crafted the true story into a popular novel.

At the same time, he must have been irritated that Lea & Blanchard had accepted Simms' book - and made it successful - while declining Poe's collection of stories. In the uncertain days that followed the loss of his editor's position, Poe's mind must have turned in the direction of writing a story that was based on a well-known crime.

Poe had every reason to feel that his skills in this area were as good or better than those of Simms. He had long made a specialty of solving puzzles and posing conundrums to his readers, ranging from coded messages to this recent success of "The Murders in the Rue Morgue." But even then, Poe chided himself over the fact that while "Rue Morgue" had been clever, it suffered from the artificial contrivance of its solution - a puzzle, he would later write, created "for the express purpose of unraveling."

Poe wanted to fix his attentions on a crime that had not yet been solved. That, he knew, would be the true test of his skill. He could not be accused of constructing his own puzzle, nor would the reader know the solution until Poe himself provided it. This would not only make the story dramatically satisfying, but it would be proof of Poe's analytical reasoning.

There is no record of how Poe chose the Mary Roger's case for his inspiration, although we do know that he had been following it since its start. He remembered the celebrated cigar girl from his time in New York and had followed the investigation from a distance. The story had gotten a lot of attention in Philadelphia and the crime had been heavily reported on in the city's newspapers. The death of Daniel Payne in October had likely brought the case back to Poe's attention at a time when he was especially susceptible to writing another mystery story.

In June 1842, Poe sent a letter to Joseph Evans Snodgrass, the Baltimore editor, with whom he'd remained friends over the years. Snodgrass had recently taken over the *Baltimore Sunday Visitor*, the same paper that had awarded a $50 prize to "MS Found in a Bottle" nearly 10 years earlier.

In the letter, Poe proposed a sequel to "The Murders in the Rue Morgue" featuring a different crime that would be based on the murder of Mary Rogers. He would change the location to France, slightly alter the girl's name, and allow his detective, Dupin, to solve the mystery. At the same time, Poe would be entering into an analysis of the real tragedy in New York.

He added, "The press has been entirely on the wrong scent. In fact, I really believe, not only have I demonstrated the falsity of the idea that the girl was the victim of a gang of ruffians but have indicated the assassin."

Poe truly believed that, through fiction, he could solve the real-life murder. For all his enthusiasm about the decision to revive Auguste Dupin for the new story, though, it likely had more to do with good business than solving a mystery. "Rue Morgue" had been widely praised when it was released and, to put it simply, Poe needed a hit. By presenting the new story as a sequel to a popular one, it could also serve as an enticement for a new collection of stories in the future.

Poe's letter made it clear that he was not hedging his bets. It would be easy to move the Mary Rogers case to the safe distance of Paris. That way, if any of the details didn't match, he could blame it on the change of venue. But Poe implied that he would name the killer and solve the case.

Was it just a ruse to make more money? Perhaps. Poe did go on to mention that if Snodgrass was unable to pay him at least $40, he could publish the story somewhere else. But, that same day, he sent an identical letter to George Roberts, editor of the *Boston Notion,* adding that he really wanted to have the story published in Boston - and raised the price to $50.

Neither man took the bait. It's possible that the price, modest as it was, seemed excessive when compared to the material they already had. At the time, magazine editors could take advantage of the total absence of international copyright restrictions by publishing any foreign authors they pleased. Although many editors made an effort to give preference to American writers, there were many less expensive options at hand. Poe's "bargain price" for his story could not compete with the free material that was available from overseas.

Concerned, Poe turned to William Snowden of the *Ladies' Companion* in New York. As you can imagine, it wasn't a particularly good match. Earlier that same year, Poe had complained about the "contemptible pictures, fashion-plates, music, and love tales" that filled the pages of *Graham's*. The *Ladies' Companion* offered these same features - many times over - and as the title clearly indicated, with the sensibilities of women in mind. Snowden worked to attract ladies of "exquisite refinement and taste," though Poe would later deride the magazine for offering neither of those things. A typical issue in 1842 featured stories and poems with titles like "Birth-Night Reveries" and "The Smile of Love," along with commentary on the latest dresses and sheet music for popular new songs. Based on this, a story by Edgar Allan Poe seemed wildly out of place.

And yet it was in the *Ladies' Companion* where the story would first appear.

Snowden had good reasons for wanting to publish Poe's story. Snowden had been a member of a group of concerned New Yorkers called the Committee of Safety, who had been involved in trying to solve the murder of Mary Rogers. In fact, Snowden had been one of the largest contributors. The committee had been very disappointed when their efforts failed to produce any results. Nearly a year had passed and yet Mary's killer still remained at large. In accepting Poe's story for publication, Snowden may have hoped to revive interest in the case and spark a renewed investigation.

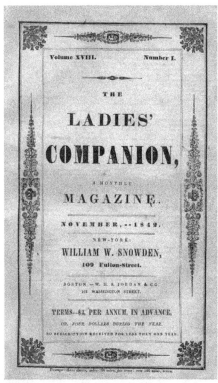

Volume XVIII.   Number I.

THE

LADIES'

COMPANION,

A MONTHLY

MAGAZINE.

NOVEMBER,--1842.

NEW-YORK:

WILLIAM W. SNOWDEN,

109 Fulton-Street.

BOSTON.—W. H. S. JORDAN & CO.
121 WASHINGTON STREET.

TERMS—$3, PER ANNUM, IN ADVANCE,

OR, FOUR DOLLARS DURING THE YEAR.

NO SUBSCRIPTION RECEIVED FOR LESS THAN ONE YEAR.

The issue of Ladies' Companion in which "The Mystery of Marie Roget" appeared. Magazines of that era were much different than today - without flashy cover art and graphics - and yet the story still became a sensation, even though it was not the magazine's usual type of story.

After completing the sale to the *Ladies' Companion*, Poe sank into a depression, largely brought on by the deterioration of conditions at home. He confessed to a friend, "The state of my mind has, in fact, forced me to abandon all mental exertion. The renewed and hopeless illness of my wife, ill health on my part, and pecuniary embarrassments have nearly driven me to distraction."

But there were more embarrassments over money to come.

In October 1842, the issue of the *Ladies' Companion* that contained "The Mystery of Marie Roget" rolled off the presses two weeks ahead of schedule. Poe's story was too long to be published in a single issue, so Snowden had divided it into three installments that would appear in three consecutive issues. Billed as "a sequel to the Murders in the Rue Morgue," the first installment was stuck between an article about the Bible and a story called "The Old Oak Chest" by Mrs. Caroline Orne.

Snowden's readers were accustomed to a quiet and morally uplifting tone in the magazine and Snowden likely took a pause before releasing Poe's graphic, blood-drenched tale. Still, even though a year had passed since the death of Mary Rogers, Snowden knew that people were still fascinated by the fate of the beautiful cigar girl. Nearly every reader of the *Ladies' Companion* would be familiar with the story, and perhaps had even visited the area where her body had been found. Most would also be aware of the conflicting theories about the case and the fact that it was unsolved. Poe's story, no matter how unseemly in its details, was familiar ground for New Yorkers, even if the action had been transferred to Paris. Poe changed the names but kept most other details the same.

And in case there was any doubt as to the inspiration of the story, Poe's unnamed narrator, the friend of C. Auguste Dupin, offered a clear statement of intent in the opening pages of the story, echoing the words that Poe had included in his letter to prospective publishers - "The extraordinary details which I am now called upon to make public, will be found to form, as regards sequence of time, the primary branch of a series of scarcely intelligible coincidences, whose secondary or concluding branch will be recognized by all readers in the late murder of Mary Cecilia Rogers at New York."

In reading the story, these "coincidences" - a term Poe uses to indicate a calculated design, rather than an accidental happening - soon become apparent. Poe introduces the working-class woman Marie Roget, the daughter of Estelle Roget, who keeps a boarding house. Marie had a job with a perfumer, Monsieur Le Blanc, and the shop became notorious thanks to the charms of the lovely young woman. Readers soon learn that a man named Bervais wanted to marry her, but Marie became engaged to a man named St. Eustache instead.

After Marie had worked behind the counter of the perfumery for about a year, her admirers were "thrown into confusion by her sudden disappearance from the shop. Le Blanc is unable to account for her absence. While the newspapers are calling for action and the police are getting ready to investigate, Marie reappears "in good health but with a somewhat saddened air." No explanation for her vanishing is offered, except to say that it was a private matter.

Five months later, Marie leaves home to visit an aunt but never arrives. After four days, her battered corpse is found floating in the Seine.

And, well, you get the idea - it's the same story as that of Mary Rogers, just taking place in Paris.

Poe was careful to insert a number of details taken from the official accounts of the Mary Rogers investigation, drawing in particular from statements by Daniel Payne and Alfred Crommelian, who are represented by St. Eustache and Bervais. He also used the testimony of the Hoboken coroner, Dr. Cook, so that his story would mirror the actual murder. He used crucial details, indicating that a strip of fabric found at Marie's waist was tied in a "sort of hitch" and that the strings of Marie's bonnet had been tied in a knot that "was not a lady's, but a slip or sailor's knot."

As the story goes on, the details continue to run parallel with the events of the New York investigation. Although a speedy solution to the crime is expected, the police soon founder. False arrests are made, and rumors spread. Eventually, the scene of the murder is found in some woods, near a public house owned by a woman named Deluc, who claims to have seen Marie in the company of a young man "of dark complexion." Finally, St. Eustache is found dead with a vial of laudanum in his hand. In spite of this, the police make no progress in solving the case - which leads them to ask Dupin for help.

The first installment ends with the narrator stating, "I waited for some explanation from Dupin." He - along with the readers - had to wait until the magazine's next issue.

As with the serial publication of Charles Dickens' novels, it was likely thought that spacing out the story would generate suspense and give Poe more time in which to turn the publicity to his advantage. Unfortunately, though, Snowden did a pretty poor job of dividing up the manuscript, cutting it without any regard for the flow of the story. The first section broke off almost in mid-sentence during a discussion of floating bodies, and the second ended abruptly in the middle of Dupin's contemplation of the murder scene. These interruptions did nothing to encourage the reader's continued interest.

Regardless, Poe was encouraged by the warm response of friends and colleagues after the first installment appeared. His spirit lifted further when conditions at home started to improve. Virginia's health had gotten better and as he wrote to a friend, "Perhaps all will yet go well."

Although Poe was still broke, he hoped that "Marie Roget" would restore some of the status that he'd lost after leaving *Graham's* and help secure his own dream of starting a literary journal. The second installment was supposed to appear during the third week in November and the third and final section - which Poe knew would contain the dramatic solution - would be published during the holiday season.

Poe was so confident of his deductive skills that he promised to solve the real-life case of Mary Rogers in the final section of his story. He wrote, "All argument founded upon the fiction is applicable to the truth: and the investigation of the truth was the object."

The conclusion of "The Mystery of Marie Roget" was going to be the talk of New York, he believed. And perhaps it would have been if not for an incident that brought the name Mary Rogers back into the newspapers - and derailed Poe's plans for a definite solution to his fictionalized mystery.

On November 1, 1842, Frederica Loss - proprietor of Nick Moore's Tavern in Weehawken -- was accidentally shot by one of her sons while he was cleaning his gun. She spent the next 10 days dying in agony, babbling incoherently in a string of broken English and German. Hallucinating, she claimed that the spirit of a young woman was tormenting her, and then made her final confession. As the *New York Tribune* reported it, Mary Rogers had come to Hoboken "in company of a young physician, who undertook to procure for her a premature delivery" –in other words, an illegal abortion. Mary had died during the operation, after which Loss' sons had dumped the body in the river and scattered the clothes to avoid suspicion.

Following their mother's death, the two eldest Loss sons were briefly charged in connection with Mary's murder –implicated, at least, in the illegal disposal of a body. The lack of hard evidence, other witnesses, and Mrs. Loss's condition during her confession were too much for the court, however, and the case against them was quickly dismissed.

NATIONAL POLICE GAZETTE.

Vol. 2. No. 27—$2 A YEAR.   NEW-YORK, SATURDAY, MARCH 13, 1847.   FOUR CENTS A NUMBER.

THE FEMALE ABORTIONIST.

Madame Restell, New York's most infamous abortionist, turned out to be collateral damage in the Mary Rogers case when it was suggested that Mary had died during a botched operation.

The police did turn their attentions to a Madame Restell, a "female physician and professor of midwifery" who had a career as an abortionist that was so well-known that some called her "the wickedest woman in New York." Madame Restell, whose real name was Ann Trow Lohman, had come to New York from England in 1831 and started on a professional path that would earn her an estimated $1 million and a lavish Fifth Avenue brownstone that was dubbed "The Mansion Built on Baby Skulls."

At the time of Mary Rogers' death, Madame Restell was also in the news. In July 1841 - just days before Mary's body was discovered - she was tried in New York's Court of Special Sessions for administering "certain noxious medicine" and procuring a miscarriage "by the use of instruments, the same not being necessary for the preservation of life." Abortion was still a misdemeanor at the time but the case in which Madame Restell was being tried had resulted in the death of the patient. This elevated her charge to murder. In the end, she was convicted and sentenced to spend a year in prison but never served the time.

At the time, Madame Restell ran her business from a house on Chambers Street, not far from Phoebe Rogers' boarding house and steps away from City Hall. The fashionable address allowed her to draw customers from every social class in New York. She also ran a network of abortion shops that stretched across the river to Hoboken.

The newspapers were filled with the possible story of ties between Madame Restell and Mary Rogers, but the *Police Gazette* worked especially hard to draw a link between the abortionist and the cigar girl. After the death and alleged confession of Frederica Loss, the rumors and suppositions assumed the tone of established fact. Although there was no official connection between Restell and Loss, it was assumed that Nick Moore's Tavern was one of the abortion shops under Restell's management. Some accused Loss of performing an operation on Mary Rogers, while others suggested that she had simply provided the facilities for an anonymous physician.

As mentioned, Horace Greeley's *Tribune* was the first newspaper to go on record and claim that Mary had died as the result of an abortion. It would not be the last, despite the fact there was no actual evidence of it.

As soon as the story ran, however, Justice Gilbert Merritt, who had overseen the investigation of the case, stepped forward to smother the claims. He insisted that the newspaper had gone too far with its reporting. He stated that the story was inaccurate and that he did not receive a confession from Mrs. Loss, who was in a "derange state" of mind.

But the *Tribune* refused to back down. Although Greeley admitted that he had made an error when saying the confession had been made directly to Merritt, he continued to insist that a confession had been made. "We gave the facts as they were told to us by two magistrates of his city," he insisted, "and we understood them on the authority of a statement made by Mr. Merritt himself to Mayor Morris."

The editors of the competing *New York Herald* were thrilled to see that Greeley's paper had botched the story. To underscore the mess, they reprinted the *Tribune's* original story and then printed Merritt's denial right next to it. When Greeley repeated his claim that two magistrates had corroborated the story, the *Herald* demanded their names. The *Tribune* declined to respond.

Justice Merritt, meanwhile, stayed out of the public fray. In spite of his denials about the story, he firmly believed that the events had transpired the way the *Tribune* had reported it and that Mrs. Loss' sons were also involved. He just didn't have the evidence to prove it.

On November 19, a week after the death of Frederica Loss, a hearing was convened in the court of Justice Stephen Lutkins of Jersey City. Mrs. Loss' two oldest sons were subjected to a grueling round of questions, designed to expose the "nefarious nature" of the Nick Moore House and their mother's role in the death of Mary Rogers. By all accounts, the hearing was a confused and disappointing affair. A team of lawyers working for the Loss family objected to most of the questions and the sons easily turned aside the accusations against them, dismissing the most serious charges as nothing but hearsay.

The hearing closed on an inconclusive note, with no charges filed, but this didn't stop the city's newspapers from reuniting behind the idea that Mary had died during an abortion. The case remained "legally unexplained," but it was "believed that the recent statement of the manner of her death is true."

Again, though, this seems hard to believe. At the initial inquest, the coroner had stated that Mary had been "brutally violated by no fewer than three assailants," but also asserted that, prior to that, Mary had been a virgin. According to the new theory of the crime, the coroner had mistaken evidence of a horribly botched abortion with a sexual assault, which seemed unlikely.

If true, though, it left other questions unanswered. Mary had been found with a lace cord tied around her neck and deep fingerprint bruises on her throat. Whatever may have clouded the coroner's mind about her "feminine region," he had been perfectly clear about the evidence for strangulation. He described, in detail, the mark left by the lace cord and the bruises in the shape of a man's fingers. A bungled abortion, no matter how horrific, could not account for the clear signs of the young woman being strangled.

The theory also failed to account for the behavior of Mrs. Loss and her sons. The discovery of Mary's clothing in the "Murder Thicket" brought attention to Mrs. Loss and the Nick Moore House. If, in fact, Mrs. Loss had been operating an abortion shop there, why would she have called attention to herself? Up to the point where she came forward with Mary's personal effects, there had been no connection between the tavern and the murder.

But, even with all the doubts and contradictions, the idea that Mary had perished during an abortion became the solution to the case for the public. Newspapers began declaring that the "mystery has at last been solved." This eagerness to accept an unproven solution had more to do with a sense of public outrage than evidence. Thanks to the abortion angle, as well as the many editorials crying out for reform and punishment for Madame Restell, the Mary Rogers story took on a new and even darker atmosphere.

At the same time, Mary herself began to be seen in a different and unflattering light. If the accusations against Mrs. Loss were true, then the beautiful cigar girl could no longer be seen as an innocent victim. She was now an unfortunate, if not entirely blameless victim of a barbaric practice. She was to be pitied for certain, but she was also a casualty of her own sins.

In the middle of all this, though, it was easy for people to overlook the fact that it had not been clearly established that an abortion had actually taken place. By the end of November, the uproar in the press had subsided, though further developments were expected. Newspapers hoped that a final resolution would be coming soon. For now, they admitted, there was nothing further to be learned.

As one stated, "This mysterious matter sleeps for the present."

For Poe, this new drama in Weehawken could not have come at a worse time. The third and final installment of "Marie Roget" - which included his solution to the case - was only days away from publication. Until the news of Mrs. Loss' "confession" and death, Poe believed that he had crafted an elegant and entirely plausible theory. Now, as the idea that Mary Rogers had died during an abortion was spreading like wildfire, Poe's conclusion would be proved false, opening him up to devastating public humiliation at the very time that he was trying - again - to restore his reputation.

The critics would be ruthless. There were many in New York that had not forgotten the stinging reviews that he had printed in the *Southern Literary Messenger.* There was also the delight he had taken in savaging Theodor Fay's book, which had also been inspired by a sensational murder case. Poe had gone out of his way to sneer at the "poetical licenses" that Fay had taken. Now that Poe had done the same thing, he could only imagine the reviews that were going to tear him apart.

Humiliation was bad enough, but if the critics tore apart "Marie Roget," then his plans for launching his own literary magazine, which he planned to call *The Stylus,* would be destroyed. In the last months of 1842, as the first of the *Ladies' Companion* installments appeared, Poe began discussions with the influential Philadelphia editor, Thomas C. Clarke, about financing the magazine. When Clarke agreed to enter into a partnership with him, Poe had every reason to believe that his dream would soon be realized. He told a friend that George Graham had recently made him a "good offer" to return to *Graham's,* but he felt so sure about the deal to launch *The Stylus* that he declined. As he wrote to the friend, "The difficulties that impeded me last year have vanished, and there will now be nothing to prevent success."

Poe desperately needed that success. His financial problems had worsened and sent him to new depths of poverty. Worse yet, according to his friend Frederick Thomas, Poe had started drinking again to excess, leaving his home and his sick wife in a state of agitation and despair. An acquaintance who ran into him during this time described how Poe begged him for 50-cents so that he could buy a meal.

Then, in November, Poe's plans for *The Stylus* were dealt a serious blow. The financing of the magazine had been contingent on Poe getting that position at the Philadelphia Customs House - the job prospect he'd ruined by being drunk.

That was followed the very next day by the news of the developments in Weehawken. That news was printed in a

Philadelphia newspaper under the headline, "New York Mystery Solved." Poe knew that he had to act at once. The first two installments of the story had already either appeared or were just about to in the case of the second part. The third and final installment, with the solution, was scheduled for the following month and may have already been set in type. If it appeared as originally written, Dupin's theories would look completely misguided considering what was now happening. Even more embarrassing, all of Poe's brash claims at the start of the story about his own solution to the mystery would be exposed as having been an empty boast.

It was too late for Poe to make any changes to the first two installments of the story, but the third and final section was still in the hands of William Snowden. Changes could be made. Poe calculated the odds, picked up his pen, and began trying to plot his way out of the mess that he found himself in.

As he struggled to salvage his story, Poe took a close look at what he had already written and then tried to re-work the fiction and facts to build a new theory. He drew a clear parallel between Marie's disappearance from the perfumery and the episode from the life of Mary Rogers when she vanished for a brief time from the tobacco shop in 1838. In Dupin's mind, the murder and the earlier disappearance had to be viewed as two parts of a single event. If so, the man who lured Marie away from home in 1838 and the man she went to meet on that fateful day in 1841 were one in the same.

In linking the two disappearances in this way, Poe opened a new line of thought. Although the earlier disappearance had not been completely overlooked in the New York investigation, the episode didn't draw much comment in connection with the murder. Poe suggested that the New York police had missed an opportunity by concentrating their energy only on the crime of 1841. Poe believed that by giving equal weight to the earlier disappearance, it would provide an entirely new way to track the murderer, which, of course, Dupin does in the story, suggesting that Marie planned to elope with a secret lover - not her fiancé St. Eustache, but the man she had disappeared with the first time. Dupin - and Poe - believed that the second episode was merely a continuation of the first event, not a second, unrelated entanglement.

But who was this mysterious man?

This is where things get complicated. In the story, Dupin points to a "young naval officer much noted for his debaucheries." Poe plucked this character from real life. In a *New York Herald* article from August 3, 1841, there is mention of this possibility. It read, "This young girl, Mary Rogers, was missing from Anderson's store three years ago for two weeks. It is asserted that she was seduced by an officer of the U.S. Navy, and kept at Hoboken for two weeks. His name is well known aboard his ship."

These three lines are the only known reference to a "naval officer" being implicated in the affair but Poe, through Dupin, fastened on to this brief mention and whipped it into a theory of the crime. Once he explained his reasoning, Dupin boldly pronounced that the murderer would be captured, leaving the reader to believe that a resolution might be revealed in the real-life drama, too.

But Poe had backed himself into a corner. "The Murders in the Rue Morgue" had offered a tidy ending. Poe had no sooner laid out his conclusions than the murdered arrived with a knock at the door. This time would not be so easy, but it did promise an even more dramatic climax - it was a story that was happening in the real world at the same time that it was being played out on paper.

Of course, this was Poe's biggest problem. Since the actual Mary Rogers investigation had failed to produce a solid arrest, Poe's story could not name a villain without deviating from established fact. Poe had sketched out a compelling theory, but he didn't leave himself a way to create a satisfying ending. Unlike "Rue Morgue," there would be no climactic confrontation and no unmasking of the killer.

When Poe ended his tale, he printed the name of the killer, but it was removed from the manuscript by the editors, or so he claimed. An editor's note explained:

> *For reasons which we shall not specify, but to which many readers will appear obvious, we have taken the liberty of here omitting, from the*

*manuscript placed in our hands, such portion as
details following up of the apparently slight clew
obtained by Dupin. We feel it is advisable to state, in
brief, that the result desired was brought to pass;
that an individual assassin was convicted, upon his
own confession, of the murder of Marie Roget, and
the Prefect fulfilled punctually, although with
reluctance, the terms of his compact with the
Chevalier.*

Poe leaves the reader to understand that Dupin's conjectures
were entirely and brilliantly correct and that the villain was
apprehended precisely along the lines of investigation he suggested.
Instead of joining in the discovery, the reader is asked to accept that
it happened offstage. Although it clearly states that Poe supplied the
killer's identity in the story, the editor is cast in the role of a censor
and removes the presumably thrilling details for unstated reasons
of propriety. It's a clever way of handling it, but this bait-and-switch
leaves the reader with a feeling of having missed an important part
of the story.

The third installment of "The Mystery of Marie Roget"
appeared in February 1843, with no explanation for the delay of one
month. The story made a startling impression on its readers, for
whom the details of the Mary Rogers cases were still closely recalled.

In one review, critic Thomas Dunn English praised the story
and noted its connection to the real-life, unsolved case. He wrote:
"To this day, with the exception of the light afforded by the tale of
Mr. Poe, in which the faculty of analysis is applied to the facts, the
whole matter is completely shrouded in mystery. We think he had
proven, very conclusively, that which he attempts. At all events, he
has dissipated in our mind all belief that the murderer was
perpetrated by more than one."

Although Poe had no specific reference to Mary Roger's
presumed death at the hands of an abortionist, his did strip away
that idea that many still had about Mary being raped and murdered
by a gang of men. This aligned well with the public perception of

the case. The previous year, when it was thought that Mary had fallen victim to a gang of criminals, the newspapers had united in calling for a more efficient police force. But now, in the wake of Mrs. Loss' death and the drama that went with it, the editorial pages were calling for the law to crack down on abortionists.

Any kind of publicity attached to the story was good for Poe. It put him back in the spotlight and restored his reputation, but it also had a few who were not fans of the writer to ask other questions about Poe.

It was not long after the story was published that people began to speculate that perhaps Poe knew more about the real Mary Rogers case than he was willing to disclose. Did Poe know who the actual killer was and just couldn't name him in print?

Later, Poe blurred the line between Mary Rogers and Marie Roget as best he could. He received many letters about the story from readers, including one that he responded to from George Eveleth in January 1848. Poe wrote, "Nothing was omitted in 'Marie Roget' but what I omitted myself. The 'naval officer' who committed the murder confessed it; and the whole matter is well understood - but for the sake of relatives, this is a topic on which I must not speak further."

This further increased the suspicion that Poe knew more than he was saying.

John Ingram, an early biographer of Poe, later added to the confusion about the naval officer. Writing about the story in 1874, Ingram insisted that it was based in fact, "although the incidents of the tragedy differed widely from those recounted in the tale. The naval officer implicated was named Spencer." Ingram didn't elaborate further, and he offered no source for the identification of the officer, though it may have come from Sarah Helen Whitman, a young widow that Poe knew in his last years.

Those who have followed up on this tantalizing clue have tracked it to a prominent seagoing family headed by a Captain William Spencer. At first glance, he seems to be a promising suspect. He was known to have been in New York in both 1838 and 1841, and his family was influential enough to cover up any scandals, as was assumed the "naval officer's" family did to keep him from being arrested. However, Captain Spencer would have been 48-years-old at the time of Mary's murder, too old to be her young lover.

However, Captain Spencer did have a nephew who would have been the right age. Phillip Spencer was a young midshipman who was also in New York during the times in question. In 1842, a year after Mary was murdered, he was hanged at sea for attempting to start a mutiny, an incident that inspired Herman Melville's *Billy Budd*. But Poe's theory required the officer to have also been involved in Mary's disappearance in 1838 - when Phillip Spencer was a 15-year-old schoolboy at an academy 150 miles from the city.

A more compelling theory places the blame on Daniel Payne, Mary's fiancé. His suicide at Weehawken certainly seems to point to a guilty conscience. In this theory, Payne learns that Mary is pregnant and helps her to arrange an abortion at the Loss tavern. In gratitude, Mary agrees to marry him but then changes her mind after the procedure is finished. In a rage, Payne strangles her but then unable to live with himself, takes his own life two months later.

This is an interesting idea because it accounts for both the abortion and for the obvious signs of death by strangulation. The problem, though, is that Payne had an alibi. He was one of the first suspects and the police thoroughly looked into his whereabouts and movements on the day Mary went missing and the following day, too.

And that leads us to Alfred Crommelian, the ex-suitor who identified Mary's body. Mary is known to have called at his office at least two times in the days before her death. Although it's plausible that she came seeking money to pay for an abortion, it's also plausible that Crommelian might have believed that Mary had fallen in love with him again. When she told him that she hadn't, he might have killed her. But Crommelian, too, had an alibi for the time of the murder. He also made such a nuisance of himself with the police during the search for Mary that it seems he had little to hide. Also, in Poe's theory, the killer also knew Mary back in 1838, when she first vanished. Neither Crommelian, nor Daniel Payne, knew her three years earlier.

John Anderson, the owner of the tobacco shop where Mary Rogers worked - and who was a leading suspect in her murder. Rumors claimed that Anderson paid Poe to write his story and shift attention away from him and toward a "mysterious lover" of Mary's. He also claimed that the case ruined his life and, years later, claimed to be haunted by Mary's ghost.

But there was someone who did know Mary Rogers at the time of her first disappearance - tobacco shop owner John Anderson. His interest in Mary seems to have exceeded that of a typical employer. Mary and her mother lived with him for a time before purchasing the boarding house and when Mary quit her job at the cigar store, Anderson is said to have literally got on his knees and begged her to stay.

Anderson's business grew steadily in the years after Mary's death. He invested in real estate and became one of the wealthiest men in the city. For all his success, though, it was impossible for him to escape from the suspicion that he might have had something to do with the death of the beautiful cigar girl. Rumors spread that he had been having an affair with her, leading, perhaps, to an unwanted pregnancy and its deadly consequences. He had managed to suppress the information that he had been interrogated by the police in connection to the crime, but the stories about him didn't stop, creating the impression that one of New York's leading citizens had a very ugly skeleton in his closet that he wanted to hide.

This seemed to destroy any political ambitions that he had. At one point, political power brokers tried to encourage Anderson to run for the office of mayor, but Anderson declined, fearing that the publicity would cause even more speculation about his links to the

Mary Rogers case. He grew bitter later in life and frequently blamed Mary's death for thwarting his political fortunes. His business partner, Felix McCloskey, recalled one occasion when they walked past the place that had once been the Rogers boarding house and Anderson cursed the young girl's memory as "the cause of driving him out of politics and belittling him in New York." On another occasion, McCloskey quoted him as saying, "I want people to believe that I had no hand in taking her off," but then added, "that he hadn't anything directly, himself, to do with it."

That's a statement that seems to leave a lot unsaid about what Anderson knew and when he knew it.

Years passed and Anderson became involved in the Spiritualist movement, the belief that the dead could, and did, communicate with the living. He confided to several friends that he was now in regular communication with Mary's spirit. He said she "appeared to him in the spirit from time to time. I have had a great deal of trouble about Mary Rogers, but everything is settled now. I take great pleasure in communicating with her face to face."

An attorney who looked into Anderson's business affairs in later years said that the murder "made an impression which he was in after years never able to shake off and which, when his faculties began to fail and old age creep upon him, lent a controlling force which undermined his intellectual powers." Anderson eventually withdrew into a mansion in Tarrytown, where he installed steel-lined shutters to ward off a threat that he was unable to name. He came to believe that his children were trying to poison him and that his cook was plotting to kill him by "putting pins in his roast beef."

Anderson died in Paris in November 1881. He was 69 and he'd outlived Mary Rogers by 40 years. At the time of his death, he was widely believed to be insane. Some said that Mary's spirit had driven him that way.

As a result of his mental instability, his heirs would contest his final will and testament for more than a decade. In was during this period of legal wrangling, in May 1887, that discussion occurred about Anderson, Poe, and "The Mystery of Marie Roget." There was a claim made that Anderson had hired Poe to write the story to draw suspicion away from himself.

No evidence exists to say this did or didn't happen, but it is not as far-fetched as it might seem. It should be remembered that Poe and Anderson were acquaintances and that Poe, as the author of the ill-fated *Conchologist's First Book* would have been known by Anderson as a man willing to undertake almost any sort of hack work for a price.

It should also be noted that in 1845, Poe took over the helm of a magazine called *The Broadway Journal* and that, two weeks later, advertisements for Anderson's Tobacco Emporium began running in its pages. At a time when Poe desperately needed money to save the struggling magazine, Anderson paid in advance for three months worth of advertisements. He was the only tobacconist in the city to do so. While this does not prove that Anderson commissioned "Marie Roget" as a smoke screen, it is certainly interesting.

There's also a bit more. Felix McCloskey, Anderson's business partner, later testified that Anderson had told him that Mary had received an abortion "the year before her murder took place - and that he got into some trouble about it. Outside of that, there was no grounds on earth for anybody to suppose he had anything to do with the murder."

Although McCloskey's memory of dates may have been a little off when he recalled this 50 years later, it does suggest that Mary's first disappearance came about because of an abortion. Whether Anderson was responsible for the pregnancy or merely paid for it is unclear, but the recollection that he "got into some trouble about it" certainly explains his sensitivity about the murder as the years went by. Even if Anderson had nothing to do with the events of 1841 -which remains an open question - he would have placed himself in a delicate situation if he had provided the money for the earlier abortion - especially if Mary died while undergoing a second operation three years later. Even if, as he later claimed, he had "no hand in her taking off," his part in the earlier abortion, whatever it was, would have branded him as a villain who helped set her on the path to destruction. Given the level of outrage about the case, one can only imagine Anderson's thoughts as suspicion turned against him.

But if the killer wasn't John Anderson, then who could Poe have gained his intimate knowledge of the crime from? Was he covering up for someone else? Or worse yet, could the writer have been involved in the crime? There are those who have claimed that Poe did indicate the murderer in his story, although he did not name him, and that the murderer was Poe himself.

A few theorists have suggested that Poe met the young woman while visiting the shop of his friend, John Anderson. If Mary did have an abortion three years before she vanished, perhaps

There were some who would claim that Poe knew more about the Mary Rogers case than he should have - either from John Anderson or some other source. Worse, some even claimed that Poe might have been involved in the murder himself! Far-fetched? Probably, but these were the sorts of rumors that followed the gloomy, eccentric writer.

Anderson encouraged her to become involved with some of the well-known and often wealthy clients of the store. Could this explain a relationship that Poe might have had with Mary - if a relationship existed at all?

It has long been suggested that Poe engaged in "romances" outside of his marriage and by the time he returned to New York with his wife and mother-in-law, Virginia was already ill. This could have driven him into the arms of Mary Rogers.

However, by the time Mary died, Poe was living in Philadelphia. He stated that he only learned of the case in the newspapers. But could he have been in New York? It wasn't a long journey between Philadelphia and New York, even in 1841, so it's possible that Poe could have made the trip.

But was Poe capable of murder? At this period in his life, Poe was oppressed by poverty and a lack of literary recognition. He was continuing to fight his battles with alcohol and his wife was dying. To his family and friends, he appeared physically, if not mentally, ill. Poe's state of mind was mirrored by many of the characters in his stories. He gave his literary creations the opportunity to indulge in crime, murder, and bloodshed and it has been suggested that these characters were simply the darker side of Poe himself. They committed the deeds that he would never dare to act on himself. Or would he?

Could Poe, in a moment of mental or alcohol-induced frenzy, have surrendered to the dark instincts that he kept trapped inside and allowed the bizarre behavior of his written characters to emerge? Could he have killed Mary Rogers?

Most would say "no," but behavioral psychologists have demonstrated that criminals often give tips to reveal their identities to the police, especially those consumed with guilt and with a subconscious desire to be caught. Was this what Poe was doing when he gave his decisive hint about the identity of Marie Roget's murderer? The writer was - just like the killer in the story - described as dark-skinned, with a full head of black hair falling over his large forehead.

Before we go any further with this, I will step in and say that this is very unlikely. As others have found, though, it is intriguing. There is, of course, no evidence to link Poe to Mary Rogers' murder, aside from that he probably knew her, frequented the cigar store, and was acquainted with John Anderson.

Even so, there are many who argue that Poe simply knew too much about the case. His story was just too detailed for a man turning a newspaper story into a fictional tale. Poe did rewrite portions of the story to fit his imagined "facts" and, as we'll soon see, made even more changes before it appeared in a collection of his stories.

But does that point to his guilt?

Did he know things about the case that no one else possibly could?

Did he really know what went through the mind of a killer?

Again, probably not, but it is interesting to consider how literary history might have been dramatically altered if Edgar Allan Poe was literally creating his own tales of murder and horror.

4. The Raven Cries "Nevermore!"

DEEP INTO THAT DARKNESS PEERING, LONG I STOOD THERE, WONDERING, FEARING, DOUBTING, DREAMING DREAMS NO MORTAL EVER DARED TO DREAM BEFORE.
— EDGAR ALLAN POE

"The Mystery of Marie Roget" garnered both good critical reviews and was well-received by the public, even if it didn't solve the real-life case as Poe had promised. Always alert to the tide of public opinion, Poe seized on the interest in his work and made the most of it. He was eager to address the plan to start his own literary journal.

In February 1843, as the final installment of the story was being released, he was putting together a prospectus for *The Stylus*.

He knew this was his last chance to collect enough subscription money to allow the project to move forward. As the answer to the other frivolous magazines of the day, Poe stated that his journal would be "more vigorous, more pungent, more original, more individual, and more independent."

Thomas Clarke, Poe's partner in the enterprise, published the prospectus in his own *Saturday Museum,* along with a lengthy biographical sketch that praised Poe as a Lord Byron-style poet and described his heroic - although fictional - exploits in Greece and Russia. Of more importance were the lengthy extracts from his work, demonstrating that Poe had become

The *Saturday Museum* woodcut of Poe that appeared in 1843. It's easy to understand why Poe hated it so much - it's ugly and looks nothing like him.

one of the most distinctive literary voices in America. Although the writing was flattering, the woodcut portrait of Poe that accompanied it was definitely not. Poe complained, "I am ugly enough, God knows, but not quite so bad as that."

Have skirted ruin with "Marie Roget" and survived, it now seemed as though Poe's dream of running his own magazine was finally coming true - but it turned out to all be an illusion. Poe managed, once again, to ruin his own success.

Within three months. Thomas Clarke had withdrawn his funding for the project, discouraged by Poe's continued bouts of drunkenness. In a letter to James Russell Lowell, Poe wrote, "The magazine scheme has exploded or, at least, I have been deprived, through the imbecility, or rather the idiocy of my partner, of all means of prosecuting it for the present."

To Poe, nothing was ever his own fault.

With his hopes dashed, Poe considered abandoning literature once again. He even briefly explored a career in law. That idea didn't last long. He still needed to write and had been writing for some time, creating a bounty of material that he'd planned to use in his magazine. With those unused writings, Poe set his sights on something new. Although he had laughed off the "present absurd rage for lecturing" when writing about Dickens, Poe began his own career as a lecturer in November 1843 at the William Wirt Literary Institute.

The timing couldn't have been better. A few months earlier, when it still looked as though *The Stylus* was going to happen, Poe had published a story called "The Gold Bug," an excellent tale in which the unusual markings of a dung beetle hold the key to a pirate treasure.

Appearing on the heels of "Marie Roget," the story featured the Dupin-like character of William Legrand, who uses his "unusual powers of the mind" to solve a baffling cipher.

The story had appeared in Philadelphia's *Dollar Newspaper* as the winning entry in a fiction contest and would become the most popular and widely-read Poe story that appeared during his lifetime. The success of the story helped to attract interest in his first lecture, which was so popular that hundreds of people were turned away at the door.

Poe proved to be an engaging orator, alternating between passionate readings of his poetry and sharp literary insights that had earlier formed his reputation as a critic. The newspapers were enthusiastic with their reviews, describing the lectures as "second to none" and praising Poe's command of the language and the strength of his voice. The first evening brought Poe a payment of $100 and this led to other performances in Wilmington and New York.

Unfortunately - it would later turn out - Poe used his new public forum to settle a grudge with a man named Rufus Griswold, who had succeeded him as the editor at *Graham's*. The previous year, Griswold had compiled an anthology called *The Poets and Poetry of America*. In it, he attempted to create a critical ranking of the country's poets, including Poe. Although Poe initially praised the work as "the best collection of American poets that has yet been made," his prospectus for *The Stylus* made it clear that he thought little of the book and intended to do a better job himself. During his lectures, Poe criticized Griswold's "miserable want of judgement" and accused him of devoting an "extravagant proportion of space" to his friends while giving little space to poets of "superior merit." Poe never said so, but he obviously felt he had been given short shrift since only three of his poems had been included, as opposed to 45 by the now-forgotten Charles Fenno Hoffman. Graham later said that Poe "gave Mr. Griswold some raps over the knuckles of force sufficient to be remembered." He was right. And Griswold would prove to have a very long and very unforgiving memory.

By the following year, the success of Poe's lectures and "The Gold Bug" had faded. He was soon broke again and Poe decided that Philadelphia no longer had anything to offer him.

In April 1844, with barely $5 left to his name, Poe decided to take his family back to New York and make another stab at literary success. He would soon find his greatest fame in the form of a gloomy, black bird.

On April 13, 1844, just a week after Poe's return to New York, a dramatic story appeared in the pages of the *New York Sun.*

> *Astounding Intelligence by Private Express from Charleston via Norfolk! Atlantic Ocean Crossed in Three Days!*

The exciting "exclusive" detailed for readers the expedition of "valiant and greatly daring men of science" who had managed to cross the ocean from Dover, England to Sullivan's Island, South Carolina, in a hot-air balloon. Given that the previous distance record set for a hot-air balloon was only 12 miles, news of a transatlantic crossing caused a major sensation.

But it was soon discovered that the story was an elaborate hoax engineered by Edgar Allan Poe. He had been trying to duplicate the excitement of Richard Adams Locke's "Great Moon Hoax" from nine years before, when the *Sun* revealed there were bat-men and other mysterious creatures living on the moon.

At first, Poe was thrilled by the strong response to the story, saying, "I never witnessed more intense excitement to get possession of a newspaper. As soon as the first copies made their way into her streets, they were bought up, at almost any price, from the newsboys, who made a profitable speculation beyond doubt. I saw a half-dollar given, in one instance, for a single paper, and a shilling was a frequent price. I tried in vain during the whole day to get possession of a copy."

After two days, when sales of the special edition had exceeded 50,000 copies sold, the *Sun* felt obligated to print a retraction. The editors offered a tongue in cheek apology declaring that they were "inclined to believe that the intelligence is erroneous," but added that they "by no means think such a project impossible."

For Poe, the article turned out to be a mistake. He had hoped the success of the hoax would announce his return to New York. In that way, it worked, but it also showed the city's editors that he could not be trusted.

Poe was determined to succeed this time around and he wanted the best for his family. While Marie Clemm remained behind to finish up their affairs in Philadelphia, Poe and Virginia found comfortable rooms in a boarding house at 130 Greenwich Street. Poe sent a happy letter to Maria, describing the dinner table at their new home:

> *Last night for supper, we had the nicest tea you ever drank, strong and hot...*
>
> *-Wheat bread and rye bread*
> *- cheese*
> *- tea cakes*
> *- and a great dish of elegant ham and 2 of cold veal, piled up like a mountain and large slices.*
> *- 3 dishes of cakes, and everything in the greatest profusion.*
>
> *No chance of starving here.*

Poe was equally excited to present New York as being a restorative for Virginia's health, as well as his own. He wrote, "We are both in excellent spirits. She has coughed hardly any and had no night sweat. She is busy mending my pants which I tore against a nail... I feel in excellent spirits and haven't drank a drop - so that I hope to get out of trouble."

But despite Poe's early optimism, within

The isolated farmhouse where the family lived at Eighty-Fourth Street and Broadway. It was here where Poe wrote "The Raven."

weeks he was out of money again. After Maria joined them in New York, they began moving through a series of always more humble lodgings, ranging from an isolated house at Eighty-Fourth Street and Broadway, then to some farmland, and finally a modest set of rooms near Washington Square. Although Poe continued his lectures with some success, he was often reduced to seeking loans from his shrinking circle of friends.

One month after his return to the city, Poe took a position at the *New York Evening Mirror* as an assistant editor and as an anonymous writer of filler material. The editor, Nathaniel Willis, later offered a bleak description of Poe's duties: "It was his business to sit at a desk, in the corner of the editorial room, ready to be called upon for any of the miscellaneous work of the moment - announcing news, condensing statements, answering correspondents, noticing amusements - everything but the writing of a "leader," or constructing any article upon which his peculiar idiosyncrasy of the mind could be impressed."

The job was quiet a step down from his previous work for magazines and far from his dream of editing his own journal. But he had little choice. Poe was grateful to Willis for the $15 per week salary he received. He would later praise Willis as someone who "has made a good deal of noise in the world - at least for an American."

As it happened, the office of the *Mirror* stood at the corner of Nassau and Ann Streets - just steps away from the site of the Rogers boarding house. Phoebe Rogers had long since closed her doors, unable to run the place without her daughter's help. She now lived with one of her sisters and the old house had been empty for months by the time Poe returned to New York.

Many in the neighborhood believed it to be haunted. There were many stories of seeing a dark-eyed female spirit looking out from the upper windows. Those who saw her believed it to be the ghost of Mary Rogers, perhaps returning to the place where she believed her mother could still be found.

After Poe's return to New York, there was renewed interest in the Mary Rogers case - from a dime novel called *The Beautiful Cigar Girl* to rumors that her ghost haunted her mother's former boardinghouse.

Poe walked by the house every day. He couldn't forget the tragedy, nor could he forget how the story he'd written that was based on it had given him a taste of success. It seeped into his writings and in a series of letters published in a Pennsylvania newspaper called the *Columbia Spy*, he pondered the unsolved mystery and his own investigation of the events.

His interest in Mary Rogers was also rekindled by the success of a recent potboiler novel called *The Beautiful Cigar Girl; or The Mysteries of Broadway*. It was written by a prolific writer named J.H. Ingraham, whose work frequently appeared in Snowden's *Ladies' Companion*. He changed the name of the character to Mary Cecilia and, unlike Poe, made no effort to solve the actual crime. In fact, he offered a contrived happy ending in which Mary Cecilia was found to be alive and well in England, having fallen in love with a wealthy British man.

This is likely what led Poe to revive his character of C. Auguste Dupin. In December of that year, Poe published a new story - his third featuring the detective - called the "The Purloined Letter." In it, Dupin is engaged by the prefect of the Paris police to recover a highly incriminating letter that had been stolen from the royal apartments. The murder of Marie Roget is mentioned in the story but "The Purloined Letter" demonstrates that Poe was still enthused about the exploits of Dupin even after the trouble he found himself in while re-working the ending of "Marie Roget." For several years, he had been attempting to convince a publisher to issue a revised edition of his short stories. Now, in a letter to James Russell Lowell, he described "The Purloined Letter" as one of his best tales of deduction. He was hopeful that the appearance of the story in *The Gift*, a popular Christmas annual, might finally bring about this new collection and feature all three of the Dupin stories.

Poe would not have long to wait but C. Auguste Dupin would have little to do with what happened next.

> *"Once upon a midnight dreary, while I pondered, weak and weary, Over many a quaint and curious volume of forgotten lore –*
>
> *While I nodded, nearly napping, suddenly there came a tapping, as of someone gently rapping, rapping at my chamber door.*
>
> *'Tis some visitor,' I muttered, 'tapping at my chamber door – Only this and nothing more.'"*

In January 1845, Poe happened to run into a friend, poet William Ross Wallace, on the street. Poe had been in the habit of reading his works in progress to Wallace and on that day, seemed more eager than usual to share his latest creation with him.

"Wallace," Poe said, "I have just written the greatest poem that ever was written."

"Have you? That is a fine achievement," Wallace replied.

"Would you like to hear it?"

"Most certainly," Wallace replied.

Poe then read the verses that he had written in "an impressive and captivating way." When he was finished, Wallace said, "Poe, they are fine; uncommonly fine."

But that was not enough for Poe. "Fine? Is that all you can say for this poem? I tell you it's the greatest poem that ever was written!"

What Wallace said next was not recorded, but other critics of the new poem were nearly as pleased with it as Poe himself was.

On January 29, 1845, Poe's new poem, "The Raven" appeared for the first time in print in the *New York Evening Mirror*. It was an instant sensation and soon became the most popular American poem that had ever been published. It went through dozens of reprints over the course of the year that followed, culminating in *The Raven and Other Poems*, a collection of writings published in November 1845 by Wiley & Putnam.

"The Raven" lyrically tells a simple tale. It follows an unnamed narrator on a night in December who sits reading "forgotten lore" in order to forget the loss of his love, Lenore. A "rapping at his chamber door" reveals nothing but excites his soul to "burning." A similar rapping, slightly louder, is heard at his window. When he goes to investigate, a raven steps into his chamber. Paying no attention to the man, the raven perches on a bust of Pallas above the door.

Amused by the raven's comically serious disposition, the man asks that the bird tell him its name. The raven's only answer is "Nevermore." The narrator is surprised that the raven can talk, though at this point it has said nothing further. The narrator remarks to himself that his "friend" the raven will soon fly out of his life, just as "other friends have flown before" along with his previous hopes. As if answering, the raven responds again with

Gustave Dore illustration of "The Raven"

"Nevermore." The narrator reasons that the bird learned the word "Nevermore" from some "unhappy master" and that it's the only word it knows.

Even so, the narrator pulls his chair directly in front of the raven, determined to learn more about it. He thinks for a moment in silence, and his mind wanders back to his lost Lenore. He thinks the air grows denser and feels the presence of angels, and wonders if God is sending him a sign that he is to forget Lenore. The bird again replies in the negative, suggesting that he can never be free of his memories.

With that, the narrator becomes angry, calling the raven a "thing of evil." Finally, he asks the raven whether he will be reunited with Lenore in Heaven. When the raven responds with its typical "Nevermore," he is enraged, and, calling it a liar, commands the bird to return to the "Plutonian shore," -- but it does not move. Presumably, at the time of the poem's recitation by the narrator, the raven "still is sitting" on the bust of Pallas. The narrator's final admission is that his soul is trapped beneath the raven's shadow and shall be lifted "Nevermore."

The poem did not have an auspicious start. Poe first sent it to George Graham in Philadelphia. Graham declined the poem, which may not have been in its final version, though he gave Poe $15 as charity.

I'm assuming that Willis at the *Mirror* printed the poem for Poe, but I doubt that he made any money from it, even after it became a sensation. Willis did introduce the poem himself, though, as a poem that will "stick to the memory of everybody who reads it."

The first money that Poe made from the poem was from the *American Review*, which paid him $9 and printed "The Raven" in its February 1845 issue. Following that publication, the poem appeared in periodicals across the United States, including the *New York Tribune, Southern Literary Messenger, Literary Emporium*, Saturday Courier, *Richmond Examiner,* and many others.

For the most part, "The Raven" was widely praised. The *Pennsylvania Inquirer* reprinted it with the heading "A Beautiful Poem." Elizabeth Barrett wrote to Poe, "Your 'Raven' has produced a sensation, a fit o' horror, here in England. Some of my friends are taken by the fear of it and some by the music. I hear of persons haunted by 'Nevermore'."

The wide release of "The Raven" made Poe a household name. but still wasn't making him any money. Despite the endless reprintings of the poem, it had still only earned him $9, while "The Gold Bug," which sold over a quarter of a million copies, brought him only $100. As he later complained, "I have made no money. I am as poor now as ever I was in my life - except in hope, which is by no means bankable."

The wake of the success of "The Raven," Poe became one of the most renowned literary figures in New York - even though he had no money. With his black suits and haunted air, he became known by the nickname of "The Raven," becoming a symbol of gothic romance that continues today.

Still, Poe believed that his fortune would come. Only a month earlier he had been a literary joke, grateful for the journalistic hack work that Nathaniel Willis had given him.

With the success of "The Raven," Poe became a sought-after figure in New York's literary circles. He appeared in public and at private events, where his verses were received with almost worshipful respect. The talents that he had earlier honed during his lectures bloomed. To heighten the effects of his readings, he would "turn down the lamps till the room was almost dark," one listener reported," then standing in the center of the apartment he would recite those wonderful lines in the most melodious of voices. So marvelous was his power as a reader that the auditors would be afraid to draw breath lest the enchanted spell be broken."

Frances Sargent Osgood, better known as "Fanny," was involved in some sort of relationship with Poe - one that Virginia apparently condoned.

Readers began to identify poem with poet, earning Poe the nickname "The Raven." With his black suit and haunted air, he cut a romantic figure. As one acquaintance wrote, "His remarkable personal beauty, the fascination of his manner and conversation, and his chivalrous deference and devotion to women, gave him a dangerous power over the sex."

Poe began to form a series of intense, usually but not always platonic, relationships with the women of his new literary circle, echoing the passing that he'd felt as a young man in Richmond toward Jane Standard, his friend's mother who had died in 1824.

In March 1845, Poe became enamored with a Massachusetts poet named Frances Sargent Osgood, known to her friends as "Fanny." Like Jane Standard, Fanny was a beautiful woman in fragile health, a combination that fit Poe's poetic ideal. Separated from her husband, she was free to respond to Poe's attention and he came to think of her as the only person who truly understood him. She wrote about him in her poems, and he did the same for her, penning a verse he called "Valentine," a puzzle in which her name was encoded in the first letter of the first line, the second letter of the second line, and so on. Virginia was not only aware of their relationship but condoned it. Fanny would later say that Virginia "imagined that my influence over him had a restraining and beneficial effect." As it happened, Fanny would later draw the attention of Rufus Griswold, the man Poe had criticized in his public lectures, adding another element to the rivalry between the two men.

As Poe's fame spread, he was offered a position as an assistant editor for a new magazine called the *Broadway Journal*. Within a month, he was promoted to the position of co-editor, with the added responsibility of contributing at least one page of content in each issue. In return, he was supposed to receive one-third of the magazine's revenues. After his experience with the magazines where he'd worked in the past, Poe was thrilled to have a chance to share in the money made from his work. It was the next best thing to owning his own magazine.

But Poe being Poe, his time at the *Broadway Journal* was brief and was marred by controversy.

In March 1845, he accused Henry Wadsworth Longfellow - fast becoming known as the most distinguished poet in the country - of gross plagiarism, launching an incident that became known as the "Longfellow War." Although Poe had always been on good terms with Longfellow and had praised him in print as "unquestionably the best poet in America," he now charged the man with the theft of a poem by Tennyson. Poe declared the theft "too palpable to be mistaken." Poe had few supporters in the dispute, and he spent large amounts of print space attacking anyone who came to Longfellow's defense. Longfellow himself, though, wisely chose not to be drawn into the fray. Unlike other writers with whom Poe quarreled, Longfellow never lost his good feelings toward Poe, dismissing the dispute as a mark of the other man's passions. He wrote, "The harshness of his criticisms I have never attributed to anything but the irritation of a sensitive nature, chafed by some indefinite sense of wrong."

In June 1845, seeking to capitalize on the success of "The Raven," Wiley & Putnam published a collection of Poe's short stories under the title *Tales*. It was his first book in five years and the stories were all chosen by Poe's editor, Evert Duyckink, a man that Poe described as having an "almost Quixotic fidelity to his friends." His story selection was a strange one. Of the more than 70 stories that Poe had written, Duyckink left out several of the best ones like

"The Tell-Tale Heart" and "The Masque of Red Death" in favor of some inferior ones that have largely been forgotten over the years.

Wiley & Putnam also published a collection of his poetry called *The Raven and Other Poems*. The small volume was 100 pages and sold for 31 cents. In addition to the title poem, it included some of his now famous works like "The City in the Sea," "The Conqueror Worm," "The Haunted Palace," and 11 others. In the preface, Poe referred to them as "trifles," which had been altered without his permission as they made "the rounds of the press." Even when his work was drawing notice, Poe couldn't help but sabotage his possible success. As it turned out, though, he needn't have bothered. Despite the word of mouth that surrounded "The Raven," Poe was still broke.

By the end of 1845, Poe's moment with "The Raven" was nearly over. With the peculiar instinct for self-destruction that he constantly used to thwart his career, he managed to sabotage almost every opportunity that he had in the wake of "The Raven."

Behind his desk at the *Broadway Journal*, Poe descended again into his familiar cycle of alcohol and arguments that had soured his chances everywhere else. Soon, his health began to suffer, and his work habit became erratic. He grew fixated with hurling accusations of plagiarism at other writers and critics, all of whom might have been allies under other circumstances. Charles Briggs, his co-editor, wrote of Poe: "It is too absurd for belief, but he really thinks that Longfellow owes his fame mainly to ideas which he borrowed from Poe's writings in the *Southern Literary Messenger*. One of the strange parts of his nature was to entertain a spirit of revenge towards all who did him service."

By June 1845, after only six months at the *Broadway Journal*, Poe had reached a breaking point. Briggs wrote to James Russell Lowell that Poe "has latterly got into his old habits and I fear he will injure himself irretrievably."

Aware that he was about to be fired, Poe sought help from editor Every Duyckink, pleading with him to buy out his share of the *Journal*. He wrote to him, "I am still dreadfully unwell and fear that I shall be seriously ill. I have resolved to give up the *B. Journal* and retire to the country for six months, or perhaps a year, as the sole means of recruiting my health and spirits."

Matters then took an unexpected turn when Briggs tried to force Poe out by buying control of the magazine. But finding the price too high, Briggs withdrew at the last minute. By this time, the magazine was barely solvent, and publication had been temporarily halted. Unwilling to suffer any more losses, the publisher, John Bisco, decided to sell the journal outright to Poe for $50 - a bargain price and an extraordinary opportunity, but Poe had trouble raising the money.

Poe was so desperate that he even sought a loan from Rufus Griswold, a man he had mocked in his lectures and often in print. "Lend me $50 and you will never have reason to regret it, "Poe wrote, adding that the magazine "will be a fortune to me if I can hold it - which I can easily do with a very trifling aid from my friends. May I count you as one?" But Griswold, along with everyone else Poe asked, were hesitant to get involved. Eventually, Poe secured the funds from newspaper editor Horace Greeley and late in October, Poe suddenly found that he had achieved his lifelong ambition of owning his own literary magazine. He was determined to make a success of it but quickly found he needed more than just the purchase price to get the operation off the ground again. He soon resumed his pleadings for cash from friends.

In the middle of this, Poe received an invitation to travel to Boston to read an original poem at the celebrated Lyceum. It was understood that a great honor had been bestowed on him, signaling his acceptance among the literary elite of Boston. Once again, though, Poe ruined everything.

Instead of reading a new piece, Poe dusted off a copy of "Al Aaraaf," a lengthy and off-putting early work, in what seems to have been a deliberate attempt to provoke his audience and his hosts. Poe had only made it through the first section of the poem when many audience members - already wearied by a two-hour speech from a politician before Poe took the stage - started leaving the hall. When it was over, Poe compounded the insult by taunting his hosts at dinner, claiming that he brought them a poem that he'd written when he was 10-years-old. There's no indication as to why Poe did any of this, but he certainly made sure that he'd never be invited back to the Lyceum again.

Back in New York, Poe began his one-man crusade to run the *Broadway Journal* into the ground. He continued to write increasingly more desperate letters to friends for the money needed to keep it afloat. But even those who cared about him knew a losing proposition when they saw one. Giving Poe money would simply be postponing the magazine's inevitable downfall.

The strain on Poe was obvious. He went on long drinking binges that left him unable to perform his editorial duties. When the money he needed could not be found, he claimed that his enemies were working against him to make sure of his failure. He blamed "one of two persons who are much imbittered against me. There is a deliberate attempt now being made to involve me in ruin, by destroying the *Broadway Journal.*" As always, Poe refused to accept that any of the blame was his own.

Poe's worries about the magazine were only second to those about Virginia's health. She had not improved, as he had once hoped. In fact, she was getting worse. In December 1845, he published a story called "The Facts in the Case of M. Valdemar," in which his fears for his wife, now more than four years into her illness, can be plainly read. The story is about a dying man, suffering from the wasting effects associated with tuberculosis and other diseases.

By the end of 1845, the *Broadway Journal* had lost both its readership and any chance for new financial backing. The magazine had been all but bankrupt when he took it over and no amount of borrowing from friends could save it. The journal officially folded in January 1846. It was the last editorial position that Poe would ever hold.

Cut loose from steady employment, Poe sank deeper into his own destruction. His drinking bouts became more frequent and his quarrels with former friends began to have more serious consequences. Rumors circulated that he had gone insane and was confined to an asylum. One day, he even came to blows with former friend Thomas Dunn English. He was drunk and was getting the worst of it. As one witness wrote, "He was finally forced under the sofa, only his face being out. English was punching Poe's face, and at every blow a seal ring on his finger cut Poe." But Poe still managed to put up a brave front. When friends tried to intervene, he shouted at them to stay away from English. "Leave him alone, I've got him just where I want him," Poe shouted.

Poe moved his family to this quiet cottage in Fordham in May 1846. It was then about 14 miles north of the city. Today, it's the Bronx.

In May 1846, Poe moved his family to the quiet village of Fordham. It was then about 14 miles north of New York City, but now it's the Bronx. Poe hoped that a more sedate setting would have beneficial effects on his health, but he did little to help that idea along.

He wrote a series of articles for *Godey's Lady's Book* called "The Literati of New York" and sealed his fate with New York's literary crowd for good. The articles were profiles of 38 authors in New York City and the harshest was written about Thomas Dunn English, with whom Poe had continued to exchange insults in the press. Poe sued English for libel, causing English to flee the state rather than appear in court. Poe was awarded $325 and celebrated by buying a new black suit.

He won the legal battle but lost in every other way. The publicity from the trial, which included stories of Poe's drunkenness, so ruined his reputation that he became publicly seen as unstable, irresponsible, and possibly insane.

By the end of 1846, Poe's circumstances were once again desperate and grave concerns were being expressed about his health. In November, a group of well-meaning friends drew attention to his plight with a notice in the *Morning Express* that read:

ILLNESS OF EDGAR A. POE - We regret to learn that this gentleman and his wife are both dangerously ill with the consumption, and that the hand of misfortune lives heavily upon their temporal affairs. We are sorry to mention the fact that they are so far reduced as to be barely able to obtain the necessaries of life. That is, indeed, a hard lot, and we do hope that the friends and admirers of Mr. Poe will come promptly to his assistance in his bitterest hour of need.

A second notice, which appeared in the *Saturday Evening Post*, was even more tragic: "It is said that Edgar A. Poe is lying dangerously ill with brain fever, and that his wife is in the last stages of consumption - they are without money and without friends."

Poe appreciated the concern that spurred these actions and was grateful for the donations that arrived because of them, but it badly wounded his pride to be presented to the public as a charity case. He sent a letter to his friend Nathaniel Willis, trying to downplay his distress. He wrote, "That, as the inevitable consequence of so long an illness, I have been in want of money, it would be folly for me to deny," he told him. But he insisted the notion that he was "without friends" wasn't true. As to his declining health, he stated, "The truth is, I have a great deal to do, and I have made up my mind not to die until it is done."

Virginia, though, was not doing as well. Her health had been in steady decline throughout the winter and the family was so poor they could not even afford extra blankets. She spent many nights shivering under the thick overcoat that Poe had worn during his stint in the army.

She died on January 30, 1847, at the age of only 24. In her final hours, she pleaded with her mother to take care of Poe when she was gone.

Poe was shattered by her death, but her long illness had already taken a toll on him. A year later, he wrote about his torment during her long decline: "I became insane. I drank - God only knows how often or how much. As a matter of course, my enemies referred the insanity to the drink, rather than the drink to the insanity. I had, indeed, nearly abandoned all hope of a permanent cure, when I found one in the death of my wife. This I can and do endure as becomes a man. It was the horrible, never-ending oscillation between hope and despair that I could not longer have endured, without the total loss of reason. In the death of what was my life, then, I received a new but - Oh God! - how melancholy existence."

This new existence was no better than the old one. Poe's habits didn't change, and his fortunes did not improve. He threw himself into work on a book he called *Eureka: An Essay on the Material and Spiritual Universe,* some kind of metaphysical work that he declared was of earthshaking importance. When it was finally published in March 1848, the book and lectures that Poe gave to support it were dismissed as "hyperbolic nonsense." Even the ever supportive Every Duyckink proclaimed the book a "mountainous piece of absurdity."

Poe's relationship with Fanny Osgood had come to an end by the time that Virginia died, but in his loneliness, Poe sought companionship through a series of frantic courtships. Many of the women that he pursued were married or otherwise unattainable, which made Poe even more interested in them. At times, his romantic overtures were expressed in various different ways at once, with predictably unhappy results.

Some of the women to whom he turned were uncomplicated and good-hearted - like Virginia or even Maria Clemm, with whom he still lived - and offered domestic stability if not intellectual company. Marie Shew, a family friend who had nursed Virginia in her final days, became the first of Poe's obsessions. She was followed by Annie Richmond, whom he described as "the perfection of natural, in contradistinction from artificial grace." By contrast, Sarah Helen Whitman, a young widow, was an aspiring poet who engaged with Poe's creative instincts and flattered his talents.

The urgent and haphazard nature of Poe's many courtships suggests that his motives were complicated, even contradictory. In time, his love life became so chaotic that after the publication of

This portrait of Poe, taken in 1849 after Virginia's death, is the most haunting of all. He readily admitted that after her death, he was "insane."

"Annabel Lee," one of his greatest poems, no less than four different women claimed they had been its inspiration.

Poe's health remained fragile after Virginia's death. Marie Shew, the nurse who was also the daughter of a doctor, said that Poe had an erratic heartbeat, and she came to the dramatic conclusion that he was suffering from a "lesion on one side of the brain, and as he could not bear stimulants or tonics, without producing insanity, I did not feel much hope that he could be raised up from brain fever brought on by extreme suffering of mind and body."

Whether Poe had a brain lesion or not, his behavior continued its erratic downward spiral. In November 1848, distraught over a rejection by Sarah Helen Whitman, he took an extreme measure and wrote to Annie Richmond to ask that she attend to him on his deathbed.

After sending off the letter, he swallowed an ounce of laudanum. It's difficult to say if this was a genuine suicide attempt or a dramatic gesture that he hoped would inspire sympathy from Sarah Whitman. Regardless, he didn't die. He vomited up the contents of his stomach and claimed that a lengthy period of "awful horrors" followed. A daguerreotype that he posed for a few days later shows the aftereffects of the incident in his deeply lined face, dropping eyelids, and haunted expression.

Poe recovered and then almost immediately began drinking again. In late June 1849, on his way to Richmond, he stopped in Philadelphia to fortify himself. Arrested for public drunkenness, he was thrown into jail, where he suffered a terrifying alcoholic withdrawal, complete with hallucinations.

Not surprisingly, Poe appeared bedraggled and worn out when he finally reached Richmond at the end of July. To his delight, he was greeted warmly there as a returning native son. Many of the friends of his youth turned out to see him and he was pleased to be reminded of happier times.

Soon, new developments occurred that had Poe believing that he was living one of the happiest periods of his live. He seemed to have everything to live for and success and love were finally in his grasp.

But tragically, that was not meant to be. Poe's arrival in Richmond turned out to be the beginning of the end.

PART TWO:
A MYSTERIOUS DEATH

5. A Return to Richmond

AND SO BEING YOUNG AND DIPPED IN FOLLY I FELL IN LOVE WITH MELANCHOLY.
—— EDGAR ALLAN POE

It was a hot day in July 1849 when Edgar Allan Poe returned to Richmond, the city of his youth. Although haunted by the memories of his turbulent disagreements with his foster father, John Allan, Poe had high hopes for his visit. He had been invited there to deliver lectures about his writings.

Poe checked into the American Hotel, his head still throbbing from his recent overindulgence in Philadelphia. Taken briefly into police custody, he had escaped a formal charge through the accident of being recognized by the judge. With the sympathetic help of some friends, including some cash to replace what he'd spent on liquor, he had been able to pull himself together and continue his trip to Virginia.

Secure in the quiet of his hotel room, he opened his valise to look over the two lectures that he had written especially for the trip. He rummaged through his clothing and personal items to discover that the lectures were not in his bag. In Philadelphia, his valise was in storage for several days, and now he concluded that someone had opened the bag and stolen the lectures. Writing home that evening in a state of utter despair, he pronounced his trip ruined unless he could recover the lectures or rewrite them.

The lecture tour, scheduled for other cities after Richmond, was not the main purpose of his trip. It was the means to an end - a way of introducing to literate audiences the news of his projected new magazine, *The Stylus*, which he hoped to finally get off the ground. He had decided that he would use the lectures to obtain at least 1,000 committed subscribers so that he could ensure the cost of paper and printing for the first issue. If all went according to plan, he hoped to release that first issue in January.

The high hopes that Poe had for his visit had been dashed by the loss of the lectures, but that would not last long. Fate was going to give Poe one more chance in Richmond.

Not far from the American Hotel was the city's Church Hill section, a comfortable enclave of old Richmond families. In one of the stately brick homes there lived a 39-year-old widow with two children. Her name was Elmira Shelton. She had lost her husband five years before to pneumonia but even that untimely death was not the worst loss she'd faced. Her second daughter had died in infancy, as had a son born soon after, both taken by disease.

As some compensation for the pain she'd endured, Elmira had inherited substantial wealth from her late husband. A prosperous merchant who had operated a line of freighters on the James River, as well as a moving and haunting company, Alexander Shelton had been one of Richmond's wealthiest citizens.

Elmira was still an attractive woman, with dark hair and deep blue eyes. Photographs created in her middle age show an unsmiling, even grim woman, but the unflattering pose was the fault of photographers who forced their subjects to sit unmoving for far too long. Friends described Elmira as having a "lovely, almost saintly face."

Her marriage, which lasted 16 years, was said to have been a happy one. Yet in Elmira's past was something that may have brought some tension into the Shelton home - if not for the

Elmira Shelton, Poe's lost love

interference of her parents more than 20 years before, Elmira would have been married to her first sweetheart, Edgar Allan Poe.

The two had known each other since childhood, when she was still Sarah Elmira Royster and living next door to the Allan family. When Poe had left for the university, they had pledged their love to each other and talked of marriage. Neither would be aware of it until much later, but Poe's many letters from school never reached Elmira. Each had been intercepted by her father, who didn't approve of the match. During Poe's time away from home, he never received a single letter from her, or guess the real reason for her silence.

The unfortunate result of this was that Sarah Elmira, pressured by her parents, was married to Alexander Shelton in December 1828. By then, Poe had left home and joined the army. They assumed they would never meet again.

But in 1836, Poe was in Richmond, making a living at the *Southern Literary Messenger*. In May, he married his cousin, Virginia, and soon afterward was attending a social function when Elmira unexpectedly encountered him with his pretty young bride on his arm. Elmira's extreme reaction to that meeting surprised even herself. She later confessed that her feelings were "indescribable, almost agonizing." When she regained her composure, though, she remembered that she was a married woman and banished the distressing memories "as I would a poisonous reptile."

That painful encounter was Elmira's last sighting of the boy she'd once loved for many years. She was a wife and became a mother. Poe had gone on to literary fame as a critic, poet, and writer.

The sudden death of Elmira's husband in 1844 brought no real change to her life. She was young enough to get remarried if she wanted it, but five years as a widow had produced no likely suitor. In December 1848, she had written to a cousin of her growing fear "that I shall never be a happy woman again."

On the opposite end of town from the Shelton house, although also on the same street, was the home of the Talley family. One of the Talley daughters was a pretty young woman named Susan, who was a budding poet with dreams of literary fame. A few of her poems had already appeared in some of the leading magazines and one had been included in *The Female Poets of America*, edited by Rufus Griswold. More recently, word had reached her that the great poet Edgar Allan Poe himself had predicted that one day she would stand at the head of American women poets.

Poet Susan Talley, who was one of Poe's earliest fans. She was also a friend to Poe and his sister, as well as one of Poe's great defenders after his death.

The fact that Poe was the only one who thought so highly of her work - and the only one who would ever think so - hardly mattered. Susan Talley was one of Poe's greatest and earliest fans. She had envisioned him as "a mysterious being in human shape yet gifted with a power more than human; something of weird beauty and despairing sadness touched with a suspicion of evil, which inspired in me a sense of dread, mixed with compassion."

Poe's sister, Rosalie, who had been adopted by the MacKenzie family after the death of their mother.

In July 1849, when Susan learned that Poe was in Richmond, and that she would be introduced to him, she could hardly believe it: "I regarded the meeting with an eager, yet shrinking anticipation."

Only a few doors down from the Talley house stood Duncan Lodge, the impressive home of the MacKenzie clan. In this house lived Rosalie Poe, younger sister of Edgar, adopted by the MacKenzies when she was only a baby. A plain and simple woman with none of her brother's mental capacity - she may have been slightly disabled - Rose was two decades older than her friend Susan Talley. But as the great poet's sister, Susan was fascinated by her.

Finally, on a day in late-July 1849, the eager Susan was given the thrill of her young life when Rose ushered her brother - who had been resting for a few days after his adventures in Philadelphia - into the Talley home.

Their first meeting was awkward. Susan, in addition to being shy had been mostly deaf since childhood and was self-conscious about it, but Poe at his most charming managed to salvage their introduction and win her over.

After that day, Susan saw a great deal of the poet, either during his frequent stays at Duncan Lodge or during one of his visits to her home. She found him to be "a gentleman, dressed always in black and with faultless taste and simplicity. An indescribable refinement pervaded all that he said or did. His general bearing in society, especially toward strangers, was quiet, dignified, and somewhat reserved... He rarely smiled and he never laughed."

Poe turned out not to be the melancholy person Susan expected. His mood among friends was relaxed and cheerful. Often, he sat for hours surrounded by young people, listening in silent amusement to their banter, now and then offering comments of his own, "tinged with playful sarcasm."

Elmira Shelton's home in Richmond

Duncan Lodge and the Talley home were the first places Poe called after his arrival in Richmond. In the days that followed, he also called at the homes of many old friends and acquaintances and soon found himself in the Church Hill section, climbing the steps of the Shelton house.

It was a Sunday morning and Elmira had been up early preparing for church. As she bustled about, a servant came upstairs to announce that there was a gentleman in the parlor who asked to see her. Surprised at a call early on a Sunday, she went downstairs and was startled to find the man waiting to see her was her childhood love. He rose from his seat when she entered the room, excited to see her.

Elmira was pleased to see him, too, but only had minutes to spare before she left for church. She insisted that Edgar call again, however, as soon as he could manage it.

The meeting had been short, but exciting - and by no means completely unexpected. Elmira knew that Poe had lost his wife in January 1847 and hoped that a chance would come for them to renew their old romance. She had even sent subtle word through John MacKenzie, Rosalie Poe's adopted father, that she hoped to see Poe when he returned to Richmond to visit the family. On his own,

MacKenzie had taken things one step further and urged Poe to think seriously about a second marriage.

Whether Poe considered the idea that Elmira's wealth would be extremely beneficial to him is unknown. It could easily sustain his new magazine and keep him from returning to his constant state of terrible poverty. In turn, Elmira would gain, in addition to a belated fulfillment of her early romantic dreams, an enviable position in the then volatile American literary community. As the backer of what could be the country's most important literary journal, she would also become the wife of its brilliant editor.

Elmira's invitation for Poe to call again was quickly accepted and he came often. Their friendship was quickly renewed, as were their romantic feelings toward one another, which may have never gone completely away.

If Elmira needed any reassurance about her prospective husband's standing in the literary field, she received it during his first lecture on Friday, August 17, at the Exchange Hotel. The supposedly lost manuscripts for his lectures, one of them at least, had somehow reappeared after another search of the valise. It may have been rolled up in a shoe or stored in another small travel case he had with him. A similar incident had happened before during another lecture trip, when the panic over another missing manuscript ended after it was found tucked into a pair of spare boots.

The audience, which had been drawn by advance publicity in several newspapers, was huge. On the platform, Poe alternated between comment and criticism and recited several poems. He did not intend to be either thorough or profound, he said, merely to expound at random on what it was that made poetry unique. He spoke for nearly 90 minutes, wrapping up with a recitation of "The Raven" that earned him a standing ovation.

The newspaper reviews of the evening were outstanding. As one paper admitted, "We were never more delighted in our lives." Another called the lecture "one of the richest intellectual treats we have ever had the good fortune to hear."

A month had passed since he had arrived in the city under less than ideal circumstances but since then, his life had turned completely around.

6. "We Regret To Learn..."

THE BOUNDARIES WHICH DIVIDE LIFE FROM DEATH ARE AT BEST SHADOWY AND
VAGUE. WHO SHALL SAY WHERE THE ONE ENDS, AND WHERE THE OTHER BEGINS?
- EDGAR ALLAN POE

On August 27, 1849, Poe took the next step in the rehabilitation of his life - he joined a Richmond temperance society, publicly swearing to never touch liquor again. This was not the first time that Poe had sworn off drink, but after signing a formal declaration of his pledge, he swore it would be the last.

And he was right about that, although not in the way that he intended.

This new attempt at sobriety was unquestionably due to his budding relationship with Elmira Shelton. Within a matter of days after taking the pledge, he had purchased a wedding ring and then went shopping for a "dress coat." In another day or so, writing home, he cheerfully remarked that the "report of my intended marriage" had become the source of happiness for his friends, the MacKenzies. Around the same time, he checked out of the expensive American Hotel and moved to the older Swan Tavern on Broad Street. It was still a reputable, comfortable place but considerably cheaper than where he'd been staying.

Poe's feelings about Elmira had been rekindled by his time in Richmond. He wrote about her to Maria Clemm in New York. "I think she loves me more devotedly than anyone I ever knew," he wrote. "I cannot help loving her in return."

The Swan Tavern, where Poe stayed during most of his time in Richmond.

Maria was dependent on her son-in-law and would be a necessary part of the new household, a fact that was understood and respected by Elmira. Knowing there might be some understandable apprehension for the older woman, Elmira wrote to Maria directly to let her know about her feelings. She reassured her about her future in a friendly and inviting letter after spending a Saturday evening in the parlor with Poe.

She wrote:

My Dear Mrs. Clemm,
You will no doubt be much surprised to receive a letter from one whom you have never seen. Although I feel as if I were writing to one whom I love very devotedly, and whom to know is to love - Mr. Poe has been very solicitous that I should write you, and I do assure you, it is with emotions of pleasure that I now do so - I am fully prepared to love you, and I do sincerely hope that our spirits may be congenial. There shall be nothing wanting on my part to make them so.

I have just spent a very happy evening with your dear Edgar, and I know it will be gratifying for you to know that he is all that you could desire him to be, sober, temperate, moral, and much beloved - He showed me a letter of yours in which you spoke affectionately of me, and for which I feel very much gratified and complimented.

Elmira went on to write about Edgar's recent "beautiful" lecture and the "fashionable" audience in attendance. She invited her "dear friend" to write her in return.

Maria replied promptly to the letter, expressing her joy that the couple had found one another again. As reported by Poe, the return letter brought Elmira the glad comment, "it is such a darling precious letter that she loves you for it already."

Plans for the wedding were made and a date was chosen - October 17. Since the couple wanted to have Maria at the wedding, and there were some other matters to be cleared up, it was decided that Poe would go back to New York, conclude his business there, and bring Maria down with him.

The circumstance that required Poe's personal trip north was an editorial commission that he'd recently received from the wealthy husband of an ambitious - but not very talented - poet named Mrs. St. Leon Loud. For the rather large fee of $100, Poe was expected to "edit" the woman's verse for a book publication. He was also supposed to write some letters on her behalf so that the book would not be entirely ignored by critics. By choosing the right critics, he could also make sure that her work wasn't ripped apart. That Poe himself would offer some kind words was an unspoken part of the bargain.

Luckily for Poe, she was already a published author so, hopefully, her work would not be a complete embarrassment to him. She lived in Philadelphia, which was conveniently on his route from Richmond to New York. He expected the "editing" of the manuscript would take no more than two or three days.

Poe and Elmira agreed that Poe would leave Richmond on the day after his next lecture, scheduled for Monday, September 24, at the Exchange Hotel. In all, it was thought that he'd need to be gone about two weeks. This would leave ample time, after his return with Maria, to make the necessary preparations for the wedding. After the ceremony, there would be a breakfast at the Shelton home and then the couple would leave for a short honeymoon at Elmira's country house. Maria would remain at the Grace Street residence. Where the family might settle for good was undecided, but Richmond seemed an obvious choice.

Their future looked bright and Poe's romantic return to the city of his youth should have been perfect, but it wasn't - not even close. There was an unpleasant thing standing in the way of his happiness or, more accurately, two unpleasant things -- Elmira's children, Ann and Southall. They were not pleased at all about having a new step-father in the house and they didn't try to hold back their feelings on the matter. They mimicked Poe behind his back and did all they could to try and discredit him in their mother's eyes. When the date was finally set for the wedding, both children wept and pleaded with Elmira not to marry Poe.

It's likely that these feelings were not merely the misgivings of the children. Some of Elmira's relatives and friends felt the same way. And who can blame them? There had been many newspaper reports filled with rumor and innuendo about Poe's character - personal and literary alike - that would not have been encouraging to anyone with personal feelings about the matter.

Either printed or circulated by word of mouth, stories linked him in one way or another with no less than seven or eight women, all of them either married or widowed, up north. Most damaging was a regrettable episode from less than a year before, when Poe came within days of marrying Sarah Helen Whitman. Rumor had it that Poe deliberately and cruelly broke off the engagement when Sarah, at the urging of her mother, arranged for her attorney to put her money legally beyond the reach of a husband. Poe, it was claimed, had broken into the Whitman house, roaring drunk, knowing that such an exhibition would end their engagement.

The truth of the matter seems to have been much less horrible, although even today, with much documentation available, it is difficult to sort out what happened between Poe and Sarah Whitman.

But none of that mattered to the gossips in Richmond.

Elizabeth Ellet

Among the half-dozen other women talked about that fall was Fanny Osgood, who had been estranged from her husband when she took up with Poe. Talk of the dalliance between the two of them was even more scandalous than the Whitman affair, because they had carried on in public while Poe was still married to the dying Virginia. There were stories about an illegitimate child - and that turned out to be true. The child, Fanny Fay, was born in June 1846 but only lived for 16 months.

Most public of all of Poe's prior female entanglements was the distasteful business of Mrs. Ellet's letters. Another New York City poet, Elizabeth Ellet had formed a friendship with Poe, writing him frequently in a scandalous manner. Eventually, there was a falling out between them and because of some remark that Poe made about her letters, the woman's brother challenged him to a duel. Incredulous, Poe refused to meet him over such a ridiculous cause and was informed by the brother that he would be the object of summary justice the first time they met in the street. To save himself being shot in public - and to allay the hysterical fears of an ailing Virginia - he was forced to send a written retraction and apology to the outraged woman. From New York to Richmond, the Ellet affair was on the tip of scores of wagging tongues.

How much of these and other similar scandals reached Richmond is unknown. There was no lack of channels for such gossip and plenty of writers and reporters who were happy to keep passing the stories along. To one degree or another, journalists of the era were fascinated with Poe and were always eager to gather news about him.

The really pertinent question was not how much did the people of Richmond know about Poe, though -- it was how much did Elmira know? We know how unhappy her children were about the marriage and there is every reason to believe her friends and relatives felt the same. But if so, why didn't Elmira listen to them?

For many readers, the answer to that is simple. Elmira was in love and she chose to believe about Poe what she wanted to believe. The rest of it was all just noise. Even if he had been involved with other women under scandalous circumstances, that was in the past. Elmira cared about the future.

Of course, little did she know in late September 1849, that her future with Poe would be very short.

Poe's second Richmond lecture was actually his third. In mid-September, he had gone to speak at the old Norfolk Academy, a performance that the local newspaper called "a delight."

Less than two weeks later, he took the stage at the Exchange Hotel before an audience that was his largest yet. With the

The Exchange Hotel, which became the site of Poe's final public lecture.

price of tickets set at 50-cents, plus the fee from the Loud commission, Poe's financial worries were over for months to come. His expenses for the journey north, and his return for the wedding, would now be easily covered.

Poe planned to leave the following morning but at the last minute, received a note from Mrs. Loud asking for a short delay. So, on the evening of the 25th, he visited with his sister and Susan Talley at the Talley home, and then went to the MacKenzies' and stayed there overnight.

The *Southern Literary Messenger* had its offices at Fifteenth and Main Streets in downtown Richmond.

The next morning, Poe saw a number of people on business matters, including John Thompson at the *Southern Literary Messenger*. They arranged for some future contributions by Poe for the magazine and Thompson gave him an advance for his stories in cash. As Poe was leaving, he handed Thompson a small, rolled-up piece of paper. "Here's a little trifle that may be worth something," he said casually and walked out.

Thompson opened the paper to find of poem of six short stanzas. It began:

> *It was many and many a year ago,*
> *In a kingdom by the sea,*
> *That a maiden there lived whom you may know by the name*
> *of Annabel Lee...*

Thompson assumed the poem was about Elmira. He knew the couple's history. Whether it was or was not written about Elmira is the subject of debate but Poe's plan in presenting it to Thompson the way that he did was obvious. He knew it would be printed as an accompaniment to their wedding. It was a perfect gift for the bride.

On Wednesday evening, September 26, Poe went to Elmira's house to say goodbye. He was planning to depart from the city the next morning on an early steamer for Baltimore, where he would board a train for New York, stopping off briefly in Philadelphia. He could have taken the train the entire way, shortening the trip by several hours, but Poe chose to make the first leg of the journey by boat - traveling down the James River and then swinging north up the long stretch of the Chesapeake Bay. He planned to be in Baltimore on the morning of September 28 and if he made his connection, he'd be in Philadelphia that same evening. After that, he'd arrive in New York on Sunday or Monday, October 1.

Elmira told him goodbye and later stated that he seemed "very sad." He told her that he wasn't feeling well but mentioned no specific symptoms. That night, she felt "so wretched about him" that she hardly slept at all.

She was still worried the following morning, so she had the buggy hitched up and drove over to the Swan Tavern, hoping to find that Poe had not left yet. She was told he wasn't there, that he was already heading north. "Much to my regret," Elmira later wrote, "he had left in the boat for Baltimore."

The two had agreed that Poe would write to her on the very day he reached home. That meant that Elmira could expect a letter within a week, at the very latest. But a week passed, and no letter arrived and then every silent day that followed caused her to become more concerned. Slowly, September became October, and the wedding date drew closer - but still nothing from Poe.

On the morning of October 9, Elmira picked up her morning copy of the *Richmond Daily Whig* and began casually reading the stories on the front page. As her eyes glanced over the column, Poe's name caught her attention. She had to read it twice before she could comprehend what it said:

DEATH OF EDGAR A. POE

We regret to learn that Edgar A. Poe, Esq., the distinguished American poet, scholar, and critic, died in this city yesterday morning, after an illness of four or five days. This announcement, coming so sudden and unexpected, will cause poignant regret among all who admire genius, and have sympathy for the frailties too often attending it. Mr. Poe, we believe, was a native of this State, though reared by a foster-father in Richmond, Va., where he lately spent some time on a visit. He was in the 38th year of his age.

It took a few moments for Elmira to realize that the phrase "this city" didn't refer to Richmond. The brief story was a reprint from the previous day's edition of the *Baltimore Sun*. Separately, the *Whig* expressed "profound regret" at the news of Poe's death, but supplied no details as to the cause or the circumstances surrounding it.

The other Richmond papers were also short on details and it took Elmira two days to get other Baltimore publications and they turned out to be just as empty of facts and details. One of them mentioned only that Poe had died from "congestion of the brain."

After being convinced the story was true, Elmira poured out her shock and sadness in a letter to Maria Clemm: "I cannot begin to tell you what my feelings were as the horrible truth was forced upon me! It was the most severe trial I have ever had, and God alone knows how I can bear it! My heart is overwhelmed - yes, ready to burst! Oh, my dear Edgar, shall I never behold your dear face and hear your sweet voice..."

As to the cause of Poe's death, the newspapers hinted toward what was believed in delicate terms, making veiled reference to the "frailties" of the artistic temperament. No one reading those words needed to have it explained that a long habit of drink had claimed another victim.

By the time that Elmira read the notice of Poe's death in the Richmond newspaper, he had been in his grave for an entire day. He had been laid to rest in his grandfather's plot in the Old Western Burying Grounds in Baltimore on the rainy, gloomy, miserable day of October 8.

Huddled around umbrellas at his open grave stood only seven people. An observer recalled the cemetery as being both "cold-blooded" and "un-Christian-like." Virginia Poe's cousin, Reverend William Clemm, presided over a ceremony that lasted all of three minutes. Poe was laid to rest in a shoddy coffin that had no handles, no nameplate, not even a pillow for his head.

Joseph Snodgrass, who was in attendance, wrote, "A grave had been dug among the crumbling mementoes of mortality. Into this the plainly-coffined body was speedily lowered, and then the earth was shoveled directly onto the coffin lid. This was so unusual even in the burials of the poor, that I could not help noticing the absence of not only the customary box, as an enclosure for the coffin itself, but of even the commonest boards to prevent the direct contact of the decomposing wet earth with it. I shall never forget the emotion of disappointment, mingled with disgust and something akin to resentment, that thrilled through my whole being as I heard the clods and stones resound from the coffin lid."

Another attendee and cousin, Henry Herring, later said about Poe, "I didn't have anything to do with him when he was alive, and I don't want anything to do with him after his death."

Within hours, Poe's enemies were lining up to pile further indignities on the dead man. On the day of the funeral, an obituary appeared in the *New York Tribune*. It began, "Edgar Allan Poe is dead. He died in Baltimore the day before yesterday. This announcement will startle many, but few will be grieved by it. The poet was known, personally or by reputation, in all this country; had readers in England and in several of the states of Continental Europe, but he had few or no friends; and the regrets for his death will be suggested principally by the consideration that in him literary art has lost one of its most brilliant but erratic stars." The obituary continued to describe Poe as a lunatic with a diseased imagination and a crass beggar prone to "vulgar fancies" and "ignoble passions." The notice concluded with an excerpt from a novel by Edward Bulwer-Lytton that the writer felt described Poe well:

> *He had, to a morbid excess, that desire to rise which is vulgarly called ambition, but no wish for the esteem or love of his species; only the hard wish to succeed - not shine, not serve - succeed, that he might have the right to despise a world which galled his self-conceit.*

Signed with the name "Ludwig," the horrible article was actually written by Rufus Griswold, a man on whom Poe had often written about with savage wit. He wasted no time in getting his

Rufus Griswold, the unhappy, jealous, loathsome enemy that Poe had inexplicably named as his literary executor. He would spend years defaming Poe, writing false stories about him, and making terrible accusations about his private and public life. He also managed to cheat Virginia Clemm out of the royalties made from Poe's works. If this story has a villain - it's Rufus Griswold.

revenge. Poe had not only been his literary foe, but was also his rival for the affections of Fanny Osgood.

Although several of Poe's friends, including George Graham and Nathaniel Willis, rushed to defend his memory, Poe himself had insured that Griswold's opinion of him be publicized for years to come. With his usual uncanny instinct for self-destruction, Poe had inexplicably appointed Griswold as his literary executor. This gave his enemy the chance to expand on the hostile obituary with a 35-page "Memoir of an Author," which was tacked on to a posthumous two-volume edition of Poe's works. Eager to present Poe in the worst possible way, Griswold made a lengthy list of his sins and offenses, many of them fabricated just for the purpose of the biography. Griswold accused Poe of being expelled from the University of Virginia, of deserting from the army, having a drug addiction, of attempting to seduce his father's second wife, and making such violent drunken advances toward Sarah Helen Whitman that she was forced to call the police. He concluded that Poe had been a man who exhibited "scarcely any virtue in either his life or his writings... Irascible, envious - and bad enough, but not the worst, for these salient angles were all varnished over with a cold repellant cynicism, his passions vented themselves in sneers." Privately, Griswold took his attacks to even greater extremes, even spreading the rumor that Poe had been in a sexual relationship with Maria Clemm.

Griswold's damning biography was occasionally smoothed out by a grudging praise for the author's prose and poetry. But his praise for the man as an artist was all but overwhelmed by his hatred of Poe as a person. This galling display of character assassination, presented under the guise of an official biography, put a dark cloud over Poe's reputation for many years.

And not content to slander his dead rival, Griswold also dealt roughly with his rightful heir. Although Griswold's edition of Poe's work sold well and went through 17 printings, he refused to give any of the money to Maria Clemm. She lived out her final days in a charity home in Baltimore. More than once she publicly complained about Griswold dragging Poe's name through the mud. "Did you ever feel as though you wished to die?" she asked, "It is thus I feel."

It was something that Poe would have understood. Four years before, as the fame he found with "The Raven" began to slip away from him, he had written what might have proven to be a fitting epitaph for his tombstone - if he'd had a tombstone, that is:

I have perseveringly struggled, against a thousand difficulties, and have succeeded, although not in making money, still in attaining a position in the world of Letters, of which, under the circumstances, I have no reason to be ashamed.

7. Five Lost Days

MEN HAVE CALLED ME MAD; BUT THE QUESTION IS NOT YET SETTLED, WHETHER
MADNESS IS OR IS NOT THE LOFTIEST INTELLIGENCE...
- EDGAR ALLAN POE

What happened to Edgar Allan Poe? How did he end up dying in Baltimore, a city that he was only supposed to be passing through? What led to his death and, more important, what caused it?

A mystery much greater than any story Poe ever wrote was born.

It's curious that only one reporter in Baltimore in October 1849 bothered to make any kind of inquiry about the death of the famous poet. This anonymous correspondent worked for the *New York Herald* in Baltimore and he filed a story that appeared on page three of the October 9 edition. It stated first that Poe had arrived in the city about a week before, after a successful lecture tour in Virginia.

The story continued from there:

On last Wednesday election day, he was found near the Fourth Ward polls laboring under an attack of mania a potu, *and in a most shocking condition. Being recognized by some of our citizens, he was placed in a carriage and conveyed to the Washington Hospital, where every attention had been bestowed on him. He lingered, however, until yesterday morning, when death put a period to his existence. He was an eccentric genius, with many friends and many foes, but all, I feel satisfied, will view with regret the sad fate of the poet and critic.*

It wasn't much, but it was the most information that anyone had provided, and it was sorely lacking in facts. From the article, readers were led to believe that Poe was found in the street extremely drunk, raving insanely, and physically battered - although the "shocking condition" could have referred to his clothing. After being recognized by someone, he was taken to the hospital but, despite excellent care, he died after a few days. It was implied that his death was the result of complications from excessive liquor intake preceding his collapse.

As we'll soon find, much of this can be disputed for its accuracy.

What the story also doesn't offer are the details that modern readers would expect - dates, names, times, locations, observations from the police, and comment on the case by doctors or the hospital. The closest thing we have to that is the diagnosis of *mania a potu*, which was a medical term for alcohol withdrawal.

As it was, an interested reader could, with little effort, find that Poe had been picked up from the street on October 3 and had died on the morning of October 7. When he was found "near" the polling place of the city's Fourth Ward, this meant a building called Gunner's Hall. The actual polling place was in the hall at Ryan's Tavern. More like an inn than a saloon, Ryan's was often used to house polling booths during elections. October 3 was Election Day for representatives to the U.S. Congress.

The *Herald* story noted that Poe's rescuers "recognized" him, but that part of the article raises more questions than it answers. In those days, celebrities were rarely recognized as they are now. There were no photos being printed in magazines and newspapers, only engravings and they weren't always accurate. The odds against a celebrity being recognized in public were great. If we add to it that the celebrity in question was horribly intoxicated, in a manic state, was certainly disheveled, and was lying in the gutter, the odds against their recognition climbed even higher. The necessary conclusion is that the person who found Poe was a friend or at least a personal acquaintance.

After the *Herald* article, there was more written about Poe but attention to the details of his death began to wane. In the weeks and months that followed, no further information came to light and no investigator made an effort to find out more. The Baltimore coroner, apparently satisfied with the verdict of death by alcohol, held no inquest. Nor did the local police feel any concern over the death of one of the country's leading writers in their city. All were satisfied, it seemed, that the poet's premature death was the direct result of his own vices.

Poe had died alone in the gutter, far from home and, while a tragedy, was not entirely unexpected. Many of those who had known him for years sadly believed such a death had been inevitable.

But not everyone was placated by coroner reports and police indifference. An urgent note was written by Maria Clemm to one of Poe's cousins in Baltimore. It brought a quick but less than satisfactory reply. Neilson Poe, it turned out, had visited the ailing man in the hospital. Since then, he had been making inquiries, but had learned nothing new. He wrote to Maria: "At what time he arrived in this city, where he spent the time he was here, or under what circumstances, I have been unable to ascertain. It appears that on Wednesday, he was seen and recognized at one of the places of election in old town, and that his condition was such as to render it necessary to send him to the college."

Overlooking important things like how and when he was alerted to his cousin's arrival at the hospital, and who told him that it was Poe, Neilson went on to describe his own small part in the events:

As soon as I heard he was at the college, I went over, but his physicians did not think it advisable that I should see him, as he was very excitable - The next day I called and sent him a change of linens, etc. and was gratified to learn he was much better, and I was never so shocked in my life as when, on Sunday morning, notice was sent to me that he was dead. Mr. Herring and myself immediately took the necessary steps for his funeral, which took place on Monday afternoon at four o'clock... If I had known where a letter would reach you, I would have communicated the melancholy tidings in time to enable you to attend the funeral...

Mr. Herring and myself have sought in vain for the trunk and clothes of Edgar. There is reason to believe he was robbed of them whilst in such a condition as to render him insensible of the loss...

He ended the letter with expressions of sympathy and regret, noting that "Edgar had seen so much of sorrow," but failed to mention why he believed that Poe had been robbed or where he and Herring - another cousin of Poe's - looked for the dead man's trunk and clothing.

Another who responded to Maria's appeal for information was the doctor who attended him while he spent the four nights in the hospital. His name was John J. Moran and he listed himself as a resident physician. When he wrote back to Mrs. Clemm, he made sure to say that he was referring to his official notes or the "record of the case." His letter - which still exists - was written on November 19, five weeks after Poe's funeral, and only one day after receiving an inquiry letter from Maria. In the letter's opening lines, the 27-

The Washington University Hospital, where Poe was taken after he was found on the street outside of Ryan's Tavern. It was here where he died under the care of Dr. John J. Moran.

year-old doctor mourned the loss of "this rarely gifted mind," making it clear that he was aware of his patient's identity.

He soon began to write of medical matters, but then, to spare Mrs. Clemm's feelings, fails to specify the cause of death. He wrote:

Presuming you are already aware of the malady of which Mr. Poe died I need only state concisely the particulars of his circumstances from his entrance until his decease -

When brought to the hospital, he was unconscious of his condition - who brought him or with whom he had been associating. He remained in this condition from 5 Ock. in the afternoon - the hour of his admission - until 3 next morning. This was on 3rd Oct.

To this state succeeded tremor of limbs, and at first a busy, but not violent or active delirium - constant talking - and vacant converse with spectral and imaginary objects on the walls. His face was pale and his whole person drenched in perspiration. We were unable to induce tranquility before the second day of his admission.

Having left orders with the nurses to that effect, I was summoned to his bedside as soon as consciousness supervened, and questioned him in reference to his family - place of residence -

relatives, etc. But his answers were incoherent and unsatisfactory. He told me, however, he had a wife in Richmond (which I have since learned was not the fact), that he did not know when he left that city or what had become of his trunk or clothing.

Hoping to rally his patient and help him recover his state of mind, Moran told him that he had every expectation that he might be on the mend within a few days and back with his family. In the meantime, everything possible was being done to make him comfortable and to speed his recovery along. The letter continued:

At this he broke out with much energy and said the best thing his best friend could do would be to blow his brains out with a pistol - that when he beheld his degradation, he was ready to sink in the earth, etc. Shortly after giving expression to these words Mr. Poe seemed to doze and I left him for a short time.

When I returned, I found him in a violent delirium, resisting the efforts of two nurses to keep him in bed. This state continued until Saturday evening (he was admitted on Wednesday) when he commenced calling for one "Reynolds," which he did through the night up to 3 on Sunday morning.

At this time, a very decided change seemed to affect him. Having become enfeebled from exertion he became quiet and seemed to rest for a short time, then gently moving his head he said, "Lord help my poor soul!" and expired!

This, Madam, is as faithful an account as I am able to furnish...

In closing, Moran again assured Mrs. Clemm that Poe had "lacked for nothing" in the way of medical care. "Indeed, we considered Mr. Poe an object of unusual regard." Word of his presence had spread quickly through the hospital and brought many doctors, nurses, and even students to his bedside. All of them had spoken words of encouragement to him and "sympathized earnestly with him."

Dr. Moran also told her that he had been so candid with her about Poe's final days because Maria had asked him to be. Otherwise, he said, he would never "even hint a fault of his" and would have portrayed Poe in the best possible light.

But, of course, Moran had not been as candid as he should have been. Addressing Poe's only family, he had no need to avoid stating clearly what he believed was the man's cause of death. He only hinted at drunkenness and his severe case of withdrawal that had Poe talking to "imaginary objects on the walls." Instead of just making it plain in writing, Moran presumed that Maria already knew the nature of the "malady" - further adding to the mystery that still plagues us today.

Even so, Moran painted a harrowing picture of Poe's final hours and that must have brought considerable distress to Maria Clemm. Aside from that, he didn't provide her with any new information but did manage to create a minor puzzle that has never been solved - his passing reference to "Reynolds," a name Poe called out repeatedly during the last night of his life. Poe had no relatives by that name and, as far as anyone knew, no friends or colleagues either.

Who was the enigmatic "Reynolds"? We'll probably never know.

Unbelievably, it would be another six years before a fuller picture of Poe's last days and hours emerged. In May 1856, a New York magazine called *Life Illustrated* printed an article written by Joseph Snodgrass, Poe's old friend and colleague. Snodgrass finally revealed that he had been the one who had taken Poe from the tavern to the hospital.

Called to the tavern by a note written by someone he fails to identify; Snodgrass describes walking into the establishment's barroom. Though warned that Poe was not in good condition, the sight of his friend slumped over in a chair left Snodgrass in shock.

He described Poe's face as wearing "an aspect of stupidity that made me shudder. The intellectual flash of his eye had vanished, or rather had been quenched in the bowl."

Snodgrass also noticed Poe's clothing and was again taken aback:

> *His hat - or rather the hat of somebody else, for he had evidently been robbed of his clothing, or cheated in an exchange - was a cheap, palm-leaf one, without a band, and soiled; his coat, of commonest alpaca, and evidently "second hand"; and his pants of gray-mixed cassimere, dingy and badly fitting. He wore neither vest nor neck-cloth, if I remember aright, while his shirt was crumpled and soiled. He was so utterly stupefied with liquor that I thought it best not to seek recognition, or conversation, especially as he was surrounded by a crowd of drinking men, and actuated by idle curiosity rather than sympathy.*

Trying to decide what to do - and apparently having seen Poe in an inebriated state before - Snodgrass was about to engage one of the tavern's rooms as a temporary refuge for his friend. But at that moment, a relative of Poe's - unnamed then but later identified as Mr. Herring - walked in. Seeing him, Snodgrass assumed that he had come to take Poe home with him but was surprised when Herring refused to have anything to do with him. He claimed that on a past occasion, Poe had been "very abusive and ungrateful" toward members of his family and Herring wouldn't chance a repeat performance. He suggested that his bothersome cousin be taken to Washington Hospital.

Glad to have the decision made for him, Snodgrass lifted Poe to his feet and found that he couldn't stand on his own, let alone walk. Snodgrass recalled, "So insensible was he that we had to carry him to the carriage as if a corpse." As the group went outside, Poe said nothing other than "incoherent mutterings."

Snodgrass remembered Poe as he normally was - a careful, neat dresser, not always fashionable but always with a care toward his appearance. Yet here he was wearing a strange assortment of odds and ends that included a cheap hat, damaged and dirty trousers, a cheap coat, no vest at a time when every gentleman wore one, and a discolored shirt that was open at the neck with no sign of a tie or neckcloth. Unable to explain it any other way, Snodgrass assumed the clothing did not belong to Poe. He guessed they might be second-hand but never looked into it further.

From there, 10 more years passed before Snodgrass offered anything further about his rescue of Poe that night. This time, he recalled it in *Beadle's Monthly*. By then, the event had occurred almost two decades before and Snodgrass made some obvious errors, mostly about dates and names, but he wasn't worried about it enough to check. But he did finally offer the name of the man who first found Poe and had sent him the note alerting Snodgrass to the situation. The man's name was Walker - no first name supplied - and he had once worked for Snodgrass as a typesetter. No details were given of the meeting between Walker and Poe, only that the stricken man managed to mutter Snodgrass' name.

Again, in this story, Poe is presented sitting in a chair in the bar. He is in a stupor because of drink, "head dropped forward." His face was haggard and now, "bloated and unwashed," his dark hair unkempt, and "his whole physique repulsive." His hat and cheap, ill-fitting clothes are detailed as before, with new items mentioned like a walking stick and "boots of coarse material, giving no sign of having been blacked in a long time."

As it turned out, Mr. Walker's name was Joseph and by the time of the article's appearance, he was dead. He had died in a drowning accident in Baltimore's Spring Garden.

It was not until after Snodgrass' own death in 1880 that anyone realized that Walker's original note had survived. Snodgrass' widow found it tucked away with some other Poe things. It was offered to the public in the *New York Herald* in March 1881:

To Dr. J.E. Snodgrass
Baltimore City, Oct 3d 1849

Dear Sir,

There is a gentleman, rather the worse for wear,
at Ryan's Fourth ward polls, who goes under the
cognomen of Edgar A. Poe, and who appears in great
distress and he says he is acquainted with you, and I
assure you, he is in need of immediate assistance.

Yours in haste,
Jos. W. Walker

The letter had first been mentioned in a story that appeared in papers in October 1849, but until this time, had only been seen by Snodgrass and Walker. It was evidence of the fact that Poe had been found at one of the city's polling stations at Ryan's Tavern. The note was proof that Poe had been found where it had long been alleged, but it also offered something else - an alternate theory about his death.

But before we get to that, we need to revisit Dr. John Moran, who, after 25 years, was able to offer more information about the part he played in Poe's death.

In 1875, a small crowd gathered in the Western Burying Grounds in Baltimore to dedicate a new monument to Poe. He had originally been buried there in an unmarked grave in his grandfather's plot. A decade after his death, his cousin, Neilson Poe, paid for a monument, but the stone was destroyed by a train that crashed into the stone carver's shop. Unable to afford a second stone, Neilson left the grave unmarked. It wasn't until 1875 that teachers and students raised the money for a proper monument just inside the cemetery gate.

Attending the ceremony that day was Dr. Moran, who was treated as an honored guest. Up until that point, Moran had rarely spoken about Poe's death, but his revived interest in the events of 1849 helped him to start a second career as a Poe lecturer. Presenting himself as the principal witness to Poe's final hours, he offered commentary on both the writer's life and death.

During the accounts of the ceremony at the burial ground, Moran was quoted at length. He was, even at that point, engaged in the task of trying to rehabilitate Poe's reputation. He started out by contradicting himself, denying that alcohol had been the cause of his death. Moran was quoted as saying, "He succumbed to an overdose of opium, which he had taken to allay the excitement of his very sensitive nervous system." Moran was actually referring to laudanum - a mix of opium and alcohol that was freely available as a medicine - but there was no evidence that Poe had overdosed on it. He then added that there was "no smell of liquor upon his person or breath. There was no delirium or tremor."

Moran went on to claim that instead of the "incoherent utterings" that he'd described to Marie Clemm, Poe had spoken poetical and mournful phrases like "Oh God, is there no ransom for the deathless spirit?"

In 1885, Moran - who had turned his lecture into a small book - provided more new details about Poe's final days and hours, naming a new source. Soon after Poe's death, he explained, he had been stopped on the street by a man named George Rollins. Then employed as a train conductor, Rollins said that he had read of Poe's death in the newspaper and had some things that he thought Dr. Moran would like to hear.

According to Rollins, Poe had boarded his train in Baltimore, heading for Philadelphia. But when the train reached the banks of the Susquehanna River, where passengers switched to boats for the crossing to another train on the other side, Poe had stayed in his seat and had gone back to Baltimore. He assumed it might be because of a storm that had come in, making the water very rough.

At some point during the return trip, Rollins said that two men who looked like "sharks" had entered the coach and took seats behind Poe. In Baltimore, they'd left the train when he did and seemed to be following him.

Moran then picked up the story:

When he reached the southwest corner of Pratt and Light Streets, he was seized by two roughs, dragged into one of the many sinks of iniquity or gambling halls which lined the wharf. He was drugged, robbed, stripped of every vestige of clothing he had on... and reclothed with a stained, faded old bombazine coat, pantaloons of a similar character, a pair of worn-out shoes run down at the heels, and an old straw hat. Later in this cold October night he was driven or thrown out of the den in a semi-conscious state, and, feeling his way in the darkness, he stumbled upon a skid or long wide board lying across some barrels on the west side of the wharf... He stretched himself upon the plank and lay there until after daybreak on the morning of the 6th. A gentleman passing by noticed the man, and on seeing his face recognized the poet...

When Moran learned what he was now claiming and why he had never come forward with it is unknown. Predictably, because of the many errors in the rest of his book, not to mention overstatements and distortions - even as to the dates and how long Poe spent in the hospital - little serious attention was paid to his theories of what happened to Poe before he was found on the street. His book was dismissed as grandstanding and a pitiful effort to cash in on the accident of fate that put him on duty at the hospital that day.

In truth, no one could blame the critics for ignoring him, especially when faced with the grandiose deathbed speeches that Moran put into Poe's mouth - "He who arched the Heavens and upholds the Universe has His decrees legibly written upon the frontlet of every human being" and "Death's dark angel has done his work. Language cannot express the terrific tempest that sweeps over me." Moran even claimed that when asked about contacting his friends, Poe replied, "Nevermore!"

It's hard to believe that he ever wrote, or talked about, any of this with a straight face - or without shame.

Still, Moran had, of course, played a leading role in the tragedy. Also, for many years, he had been a resident of Baltimore, available to hear, and be told, many things about Poe's last days - even if much of it was rumor and tall tale.

And Moran was not the only person who claimed that Poe left Baltimore and then came back again. In 1877, William Gill wrote in the first attempt at a Poe biography, that Poe had stopped for a drink or two before boarding the Philadelphia train. Drunk on the train, the conductor assumed that he had friends or family in Baltimore and brought him back to the city.

Where William Gill had learned this version of the story is unknown - he didn't reveal his sources.

One of the lingering mysteries in the wake of Poe's death was what had become of his luggage. He had a small traveling trunk with him when he left Richmond, a sturdy, metal-wrapped wooden case that was about two feet wide. Neilson Poe was unable to find it immediately after his cousin's death.

The trunk and its whereabouts were among the first things people thought of when trying to figure out what happened. It was thought that the location of the trunk could indicate something about Poe's movements in his last days - days that remained a blank.

It was Dr. Moran who succeeded where Neilson Poe failed. In late October, he tracked it down in storage at a hotel called Bradshaw's, which was near the train station from which Poe would leave Baltimore. He promptly gave it to Neilson Poe, who sent it on to Maria Clemm.

Unfortunately, the contents of the trunk revealed nothing about Poe's fate - there were some manuscripts, books, clothing, and some personal items. The contents were so innocuous that no one ever even made a list, but judging from separate references, those items can be taken as certain.

As it turned out, the contents of the trunk didn't turn out to be nearly as important as where the trunk was found. That would be a key to one of the theories that would soon emerge about Poe's fate.

But a real investigation into what happened to Edgar Allan Poe has to begin with his five lost days. If Poe was found in Baltimore on October 3, having departed early in the morning from Richmond on September 27, where had he been during those missing days, and who was he with? There were only a few vague and unsupported rumors that floated around years later, but none of them led anywhere.

That puzzle tantalized researchers for at least two decades before anyone began to try and make a real effort to solve it. In September 1872, an article appeared in *Harper's Magazine* that while it offered no evidence, it made some strong claims about at least a few of the lost days. The article was written by R.H. Stoddard and it offered a short, unsympathetic look at Poe's life, but concluded with the following:

> *The facts, as far as they can be ascertained, appear to be these: He arrived at Baltimore safely, but between trains unfortunately he took a drink with a friend, the consequence of which was that he was brought back from Havre de Grace by the conductor of the Philadelphia train, in a state of delirium. It was on the eve of an exciting municipal election, and as he wandered up and down the streets of Baltimore he was seized by the lawless agents of some political club, and shut up all night in a cellar. The next morning he was taken out in a state of frenzy, drugged, and made to vote in eleven different wards. The following day he was found in a back room of a "headquarters" and removed to a hospital.*

Stoddard, who was a leading New York editor and writer at the time, never revealed how or where he obtained this information. But the lack of support for this unusual claim didn't seem to matter - no one argued about it and many just accepted it as truth.

Two years later, in August 1874, this theory appeared again, this time in an article for *The Southern Magazine,* which was published in Baltimore. In this article, William Baird, wrote a lengthy piece on Poe's life and repeats the claim about election violence from Stoddard's article. It was again presented as established fact.

This sequence of events is a good example of how a story can be picked up and told over and over again until it's accepted as the truth. Neither writer offered any measure of corroborating details for what was a fairly radical solution to the mystery, which was being offered many years after the fact. It was certainly a possible sequence of events, but where did it come from?

Behind the scenes, the editor of *The Southern Magazine*, William Hand Browne, supplied the information left out of the article to John Ingram, who was then researching what turned out to be the first generally reliable Poe biography. He sent Ingram a copy of the Baird article with an attached note:

> *At that time, and for years before and after, there was an infamous custom in this and other cities, at election time, of "cooping" voters. That is, gangs of men picked up, inveigled, or even carried off by force, men whom they found in the streets (generally the poor, friendless, or strangers) and transported them to cellars in various slums of the city, where they were kept under guard, threatened, maltreated if they attempted to escape, often robbed, and always compelled to drink whiskey (frequently drugged) until they were stupefied and helpless.*
>
> *At the election these miserable wretches were brought up to the polls in carts or omnibuses, under guard, and made to vote with tickets in their hands. Death from ill-treatment was not very uncommon. The general belief here is, that Poe was seized by one of these gangs (his death happening just at election time; an election for sheriff took place on October 4), "cooped," stupefied with liquor, dragged out and voted, then turned adrift to die...*

Browne offered some corroboration for this theory by way of a volume about Baltimore history that had been published that year. In it, the author J.T. Scharf, wrote about the elections, "In addition to ordinary acts of riot and intimidation, honest gentlemen, as well as unfortunate wretches, were frequently seized and 'cooped' in vile dens, drugged, stupefied with whiskey, and then carried round and 'voted' in ward after ward, the police offering no opposition, and the judges receiving the votes."

Browne added that this custom had gone on for years, but things eventually became so bad that reformers armed themselves, took to the streets at election time, and put an end to the violence and fraud.

Again, this was a plausible theory about what happened to Poe, but there was no actual evidence that it had anything to do with his missing days.

It turned out that the originator of the idea that Poe was an unfortunate victim of election violence was an old friend and colleague in Richmond, *Messenger* editor John R. Thompson. He first suggested this idea in a lecture, "The Genius and Character of Edgar Allan Poe," which he performed many times in cities North and South during the late 1860s and until his death in April 1873. One of the cities where he spoke was Baltimore, where interest in Poe was always high, especially regarding his death. He was also a friend of fellow editor, William Hand Browne and, widening the circle, was also friends with R.H. Stoddard, who used Thompson as a source for his *Harper's* article.

John Thompson, in addition to being the originator of the theory, was also the one who - through contacts at two different publications - put it into print. John Ingram hoped to be the first formal biographer to offer the cooping theory in his book but was beaten by a competitor, William Gill, when he published his own book about Poe's life in 1877. Drawing on the Baird article, Gill presents the story as if the facts were unquestioned - Poe was seized by political gangs, locked in a cell overnight where he was drugged, then taken out the next morning and "made to repeat votes at eleven different wards. The "eleven wards" had reached Baird through Stoddard from Thompson, who never said how he knew, or could have known, that precise number.

Gill's book did poorly, dismissed as an anemic effort, and so Ingram still had his chance to present the theory to a wider audience. He took full advantage of it.

Using material on Poe's death that he was sent from Baltimore, he expanded it from various other sources and published his book in 1880. After that, the cooping theory of Poe's death became more or less fixed in literature. Even though it's often been denied in whole or in part, the theory has never gone away altogether and likely never will.

The section in Ingram's book read:

> *Upon his arrival, he gave his trunk to a porter to convey it, it is stated, to the cars which were timed to leave in an hour or so for Philadelphia, whilst he sought some refreshment. What happened now is still shrouded in mystery: before leaving Richmond the poet had complained of indisposition; of chilliness, and of exhaustion, and it is just possible that the increase of these symptoms may have enticed him into breaking his pledge, or into resorting to some deleterious drug.*
>
> *Be the cause whatever it may, it now appears to have become the fixed belief of the Baltimoreans, that the unfortunate poet, while in a state of temporary mania or stupor, fell into the hands of a gang of ruffians who were scouring the streets in search of victims. Wednesday the 3rd of October was election day for members of Congress in the state of Maryland, and it is the general supposition that Poe was captured by an electioneering band, "cooped," drugged, dragged to the polls, and then, after having voted the ticket placed in his hand, was ruthlessly left in the street to die. For the truth of this terrible tale there appears too great a probability.*

Ingram couldn't help but add to the story, having Poe flag down a porter to convey his trunk to the train station while he looked for "refreshment" - which is a code word for liquor - was all unproven and embellished. He lends credence to the "cooping" theory but neatly avoids taking credit for it, shuffling it off to the "fixed belief" of Baltimore residents. However, he closes by saying it's a "probability."

At this point, the cooping theory has been around for more than a decade without the benefit of any real evidence linking Poe to the practice. The only real connection seems to have been that he was found near a polling place. This had been revealed in the earliest reports of Poe's death, but it wasn't considered significant until 1874, when writers began to emphasize it.

Then, in 1880, with the discovery of the original Walker note, it seemed the theory had been clinched. Some even assumed that Ryan's Tavern itself had been an "election-coop," but this is nearly impossible. The idea that a designated polling place had a bunch of drugged and liquored men huddled in the basement waiting their turn to vote was ridiculous. The place was monitored that day - according to newspapers - by three election judges and an increased police patrol.

But the letter did assure the placement of the cooping theory in every biographical piece about Poe that appeared. An article was published in the *New York Herald* in March 1881 -- written by Edward Spencer from the *Baltimore Sun,* working closely with editor Browne - that tried to track down the elusive Joseph Walker. It was quickly discovered that Walker had died in a drowning accident years before, leaving behind no information about his fateful encounter with Poe. Snyder believed that, based on the wording in his note to Snodgrass, Walker didn't know Poe and didn't recognize him when he found him in the gutter at Ryan's. But if that was the case, why would he stop and talk to an inebriated man lying in the street?

Undaunted by logic, Spencer began digging, looking for the supposed coop himself, even hoping to turn up some of its former occupants. Five months before the publication of the article by the *Herald,* Browne wrote that Spencer was "hunting up all about Ryan's place and will try and see if any of Poe's fellow prisoners in that den can now be found. He will then prepare a paper for one of the magazines." The article, when it appeared, was a long one, dealing with other elements of Poe's life, in addition to the Walker letter. But what he had to say about Walker and the cooping business was the most compelling part of it.

Pointing out that Ryan's was only a door or two away from High Street, Spencer noted that Snodgrass lived on High Street, only two blocks away from the tavern. Probably, he suggested, it was this "immediate proximity as much as anything else which prompted Walker to send for him" instead of someone else. It was a good point, but it assumed that Walker knew where Snodgrass lived and it leaves out the fact that Poe, when questioned by Walker, managed to say Snodgrass's name.

But what really got Spencer's attention was the description of Poe that Snodgrass gave in his *Beadle's* article 14 years earlier. Quoting from the Walker note, Spencer indignantly rejects the Snodgrass phrase -- "in a state of beastly intoxication and evident destitution" - contrasting it with Walker's milder description of "a gentleman rather the worse for wear," who was in need of assistance. Walker, Spencer decided, had found only "a man so ill as to excite" the sympathy of a passerby. Yet Snodgrass saw him as "a drunken and penniless loafer."

With that, Spencer proceeds to offer the reader a number of facts mixed with guesses that are calculated to leave no doubt about the cooping theory and that being the reason for his death. He begins by permitting himself one small assumption that Poe, after arriving in Baltimore, would have stopped at the United States Hotel for refreshment while waiting for the evening train to Philadelphia. It's not a bad guess - the hotel was directly opposite the train station at the time.

Spencer wrote:

> *Eight blocks east of the hotel was High Street, and in the rear of an engine-house in this vicinity the "Fourth Ward Club," a notorious Whig organization, had their "coop." There was no registry of voters at this time in Baltimore, and almost anyone who could vote who was willing to face the ordeal of a "challenge," and the oath administered by the judge of elections.*

The roughs of the period, instead of acting as rounders themselves, used to capture and "coop" innocent strangers and foreigners, drug them with bad whiskey and opiates, and send them round to different voting places under custody of one or two of their party.

If the writer's memory does not play him a trick, the coop of the Democrats on Lexington Street, near Eutaw, in the rear of the New Market engine-house, had 75 prisoners, while that of the Whigs, on High Street, had 130 to 140.

The prisoners in these "coops," chiefly foreigners, strangers, and countrymen, fared wretchedly. They were often, at the outstart and in the most unexpected way, drugged with opiates and such other delirifacients as would be most likely to keep them from being troublesome.

They were thrust into cellars and backyards, and kept under lock and key, without lights, without beds, without provisions for decency, without food. Only one thing they were supplied with, and that was a significant deluge of whiskey to keep their brains all the time sodden.

The Whig coop in the Fourth Ward on High Street was within two squares of the place where Poe was "found." It is altogether possible that Poe was cooped, and his outlaw custodians, discovering too late the disastrous effects of their infamous decoctions upon the delicate tissues and convolutions of his finely organized brain, sought to repair some of the damage they had done, and caused inquiry to be made for the friends of the man they had murdered. Too late!

How the sympathetic Walker fit into this wild tale is unclear. Spencer's phrasing could just be poor - and it's obvious he was getting paid by the word - but he seems to actually place Walker among Poe's "outlaw custodians." Or at least it makes it seem as though he was aware of what had happened to Poe before he was found. It's an almost libelous charge to make, but Spencer was in the clear since Walker had been dead for years.

After Spencer and Ingram, the cooping story remained in Poe's biography for the next 75 years. For some, it was a strong possibility, for others nearly certain, especially for those who wanted to move the blame for what happened to Poe to a third party. They were eager to make it clear that Poe couldn't possibly have gotten drunk on his own and experienced one of his infamous blackouts.

Eventually, though, the cooping theory started to fade away. It had not been contradicted by any clear evidence or string argument against it, rather it seemed that Poe's biographers just became bored with it. Its last full-fledged appearance was in a 1941 biography by A.H. Quinn. After that, it dwindled away and soon, scholarly writings about Poe called the theory "fanciful." In the excellent Kenneth Silverman biography of Poe that came out in 1991, it gets no mention at all. His narrative jumps from the day of Poe's departure from Richmond on September 27 to the afternoon when he was found. There is only a blank for the days between. Author John Evangelist Walsh, in his 2000 book, has his own theories about Poe's demise but none of them involve cooping.

But he does point out the odd thing about all the research that was done into the cooping theory is that none of the proponents of it make mention of what the newspapers said about the day's election activities. If there was so much cooping going on in the city - apparently hundreds of unlucky men being rounded up and badly treated - did any reporters realize what was going on? Did anyone complain to the police?

As it happens, the *Baltimore Sun* for October 4 said that all the rain on the previous day had kept voter turnout low for the election:

> *There was little excitement in the city during the day, and not much more at night. The election passed off quite harmoniously, and we heard of no disturbances at the polls or elsewhere. The voting progressed steadily, exhibiting only the impulses*

incident to the variations of weather, and the occasional appearance of voters by the dozen or score. As the returns begin to come in, the successful party became a little musical, and throughout the early part of the evening bonfires illuminated the streets, and discharges of gunpowder in various forms celebrated the victory.

So, if it was happening, the newspapers, police, and election officials were unaware of it. There doesn't seem to be any evidence that it was happening in 1849, especially not to Edgar Allan Poe.

What is the answer behind Poe's missing days?

And why would such an unusual claim be made in the first place?

8. The Death of "The Raven"

THANK HEAVEN! THE CRISIS — THE DANGER IS PAST, AND THE LINGERING ILLNESS,
IS OVER AT LAST — AND THE FEVER CALLED "LIVING," IS CONQUERED AT LAST.
- EDGAR ALLAN POE

While I wouldn't consider myself a scholar when it comes to Edgar Allan Poe - or a scholar on much of anything, really - I have had a lifelong affinity for the writer and poet. You might say that I was born to have one because my middle name is "Allan," in honor of the mysterious author. But despite my lack of scholarly credentials, I have always been fascinated with the various theories of what happened to Poe when he left Richmond in late September. There are certainly some very strange elements to the story that have never been fully addressed and I think that now that we have moved beyond "cooping," we should delve a little deeper into the alternate theories of Poe's final days.

For many years, it was thought that the last person to see Poe alive in Richmond was his fiancé, Elmira, who had watched him leave her home and walk towards the Swan Tavern so he could prepare to leave on his journey early the next morning. But shortly after the turn of the last century, reliable information appeared that placed Poe somewhere else in Richmond on that night.

After leaving Elmira, he stopped in at the office of Dr. John Carter, which was about a 10-minute walk from the Shelton home. This was revealed by Dr. Carter himself in his old age, writing for *Lippincott's Magazine* in November 1902.

Dr. John Carter in 1902, when he wrote about Poe's last night in Richmond.

Carter had been a friend of the MacKenzie family for many years and had met Poe socially many times during his stay in the city. No one knows why Poe stopped to see Carter that night. Carter later said only that the office provided him a "resting place" between Elmira's home and the Swan. He also never mentioned why the office was open so late in the evening.

Poe lingered for a while at Carter's office. The two men talked but nothing was mentioned about medical attention. Years later, it was claimed that Carter advised Poe to stay in Richmond for a few extra days, postponing his trip, because he'd been feeling ill. There is no evidence of this in Carter's own recollections, though.

Eventually, Poe said that he was going to stroll to a local restaurant on Main Street called Sadler's, which was about three blocks away. Leaving the office, he took not his own walking stick, but Dr. Carter's. In the South in those days, most gentlemen sported a cane and Poe readily adopted the practice. Carter's cane was a little different than the usual walking stick. It had a handle that twisted and when turned, a sword was released from where it was concealed inside of the shaft. It was both fashionable and deadly.

Dr. Carter's revelations about that night appeared in the closing paragraphs of the story. At the time of the incident, he was a young doctor of only 24. He had not seen Poe for several days leading up to that night but was surprised when he stopped by. After chatting and announcing that he planned to go to Sadler's, Poe left, taking Carter's cane with him.

> *From this manner of departure, I inferred that he expected to return shortly, but did not see him again, and was surprised to learn next day that he had left Baltimore by the early morning boat. I then called on Sadler, who informed me that Poe had left his house at exactly twelve that night, starting for the Baltimore boat in company with several companions whom he had met at Sadler's, and giving as a reason therefor the lateness of the hour and the fact that the boat was to leave at four o'clock.*
>
> *According to Sadler, he was in good spirits and sober, though it is certain that he had been drinking and that he seemed oblivious of his baggage, which had been left in his room at Swan Tavern.*

Carter's actions the next morning in asking after Poe were fortunate because it produced the only contemporary firsthand account that Poe actually did leave town that morning, by steamer as he had planned. His source for the information, the restaurant proprietor Sadler, is also important because Poe was well-known to him as a regular customer.

But the last part of Carter's statement seems amiss. According to Sadler, Poe was sober when he left the restaurant. For some reason, though, Carter states that it was "certain he had been drinking." How was this a certainty? Carter wasn't with Poe at the restaurant - Sadler was, and he said that Poe was sober. It's likely that Carter knew of Poe's problems with alcohol and, after hearing all the stories of how he was found drunk and in a stupor in

Baltimore, he assumed he must have been drinking before he ever left Richmond.

He also based this judgement on Poe leaving his luggage behind at the Swan. But we do know that Poe had his traveling trunk with him in Baltimore, so he didn't get drunk and forget his luggage. He likely left some of his belongings behind at the Swan because he planned to return there after his trip to Philadelphia and New York. Poe would have kept the room as a place to stay before the wedding. He was feeling flush with a recent influx of money and keeping the room reserved would not have seemed an inconvenience at the time. It would be waiting for him when he got back in town.

But here's the more ominous part of the story - who were the "several companions" that joined Poe while he ate and then escorted him to his boat when he left the restaurant at midnight?

Their identities are never mentioned - probably because they were unimportant. I think the mention of these companions have muddied the waters over the years and likely had nothing to do with what happened in Baltimore.

I believe that a big part of the mystery of Poe's death can be solved if we can understand how he ended up wearing someone else's clothing in Baltimore. It's not the answer to everything, but it's a start.

We do know from the statements of both Walker and Snodgrass that Poe was wearing cheap clothing and at least some of it was not his own. In fact, the strange clothing was what gave Snodgrass the greatest shock when he found Poe in that dingy barroom. A shabby appearance was totally at odds with what was known of Poe's usual dress. Even when he was low on funds, he still managed to make sure that his suit was neat and carefully brushed. In New York, Virginia had spent many hours repairing his clothing and making sure that he looked respectable.

But this was not the first time that Poe's friends found him in unusual, dirty, disheveled clothing. It had happened twice before and under very strange -- even terrifying -- circumstances. They occurred not in October 1849, but in the early days of July, just before he arrived in Richmond. Curiously, one of them even reveals his own deliberate effort to change his appearance by disguising himself.

Both incidents occurred during his stopover in Philadelphia where, as discussed earlier, Poe fell victim to one of his periodic drinking sprees. I believe it was his last drinking spree, but we'll come back to that.

Both incidents involved Poe being aided by friends, with the stories put on record by the friends themselves. How the two accounts fit together is the first question to be answered, especially in regard to the evident emphasis on Poe's appearance.

Before we get to the first account, keep in mind that Poe had already done great damage to himself with his drinking sprees in the past, not only professionally and personally, but physically as well. It has been established that Poe had an unusual reaction to liquor. Only a small amount would cause him to become very drunk. A large amount sent him into blackouts that left him incoherent in the street, unaware of where he was or even who he was, and unable to function. He was subject to delirium tremors and violent reactions to alcohol withdrawal. This suggests that by the summer of 1849, Poe was having serious health issues that only a complete halt to his drinking would have eased. He had arrived in Richmond - after his adventures in Philadelphia - in a fragile state of mind and body but he began to recover after joining the temperance society and renewing his romance with Elmira.

And then came Baltimore.

But let's look now at what happened before Richmond.

The first of Poe's friends to go on record about the incidents was George Lippard, age 27, a writer, and old acquaintance of Poe. Just four years after Poe's death, Lippard recalled an unexpected visit from Poe that occurred in his office in Philadelphia "on a hot summer day," no other date mentioned. Poe was, Lippard said, in a state of severe despondency, "poorly clad and with but one shoe on his feet. He came stealthily upstairs, as if conscious that he was an intruder anywhere."

Seating himself in a chair, Poe blurted out to his surprised friend that "he had no bread to eat - no place to sleep - not one friend in God's world." This was the first time that Lippard had seen Poe in at least five years, when the poet had still been living in the city. Painfully recalling happier days with his friend, he felt instant sympathy for the downtrodden Poe, so "shabbily clad," as he said, who was now looking for a small loan to pay his way to Richmond. A struggling writer with his own financial woes, Lippard didn't have a penny to spare. Poe suggested that he might ask on his behalf to some other editors and publishers in the city and Lippard quickly agreed.

Poe called after him. "Tell them I am sick, that I haven't got a bed to sleep upon. That I only want to get out of Philadelphia... For God's sake, don't fail me! You're my last hope!"

Poe's friend in Philadelphia, George Lippard

While Poe waited in Lippard's office, his friend called on several mutual acquaintances and men who knew Poe, either personally or through his writings. Five of them made contributions.

The next day, a recovered Poe, now calmer and filled with gratitude, was accompanied to his train by Lippard and one or two other men who weren't named. They put him on board and "never saw him again."

Lippard had called Poe's clothing both poor and shabby, but it's unknown exactly what he meant by that. Were they good clothes that were dirty and in disrepair, or cheap coat and trousers that were below the standards of a gentleman? The writings give no clue.

There is no question that Poe's request for Lippard to go around soliciting funds for him was strange. Why didn't Poe do it himself, rather than impose on someone he hadn't seen in years? Why was it necessary for Poe to remain behind in his office and wait for him to return? Was he embarrassed about his appearance,

The other friend that Poe turned to for help in Philadelphia, John Sartain.

embarrassed about begging for money, or was there some other reason?

And that final question brings us to the other incident that occurred in Philadelphia around that time. This one involved a publisher named John Sartain, and this incident is much more complicated - and confusing - than the other. It can be unraveled, though, but only a step at a time. To try and understand it, we have to look at Sartain's original statement. That is, however, another complication. Sartain told the story of what happened several times, at more or less length, during a 25-year period.

In the summer of 1849, Sartain was 41-years-old and had known Poe for at least a decade. The two had first met when working together on *Graham's Magazine* in Philadelphia. Sartain was an engraver and Poe was an editor. Later, their careers went in different directions, but they remained on friendly terms, Sartain especially showing great respect for Poe and his talents. When the two men met again in 1849, Sartain was the proprietor of the influential *Union Magazine* and was well-known in the literary world. Works by some of the most respected writers in the country had appeared in the pages of his magazine.

Sartain first wrote about the incident with Poe in 1875, when he recalled it in detail for biographer William Gill. The story then appeared in *Lippincott's Magazine* in 1889, in the *Philadelphia Press* in 1892, in a lengthy account in the *Philadelphia Record* - reprinted in other papers - in 1893, and finally, in a 10-page section of Sartain's autobiography, published in 1899.

To understand the entire incident, it's necessary to look at all five sources, starting with the most complete one, which appeared in *Lippincott's*. I know what you may be thinking, but trust me, it's worth it - this is really strange.

Sartain details the incident, but an attentive reader will soon see that he is confused about some parts of the story and in some spots, even contradicts himself. As I said, this one is strange, so don't skip over anything.

The last time I saw Mr. Poe was in 1849, and then under such peculiar and fearful conditions that it can never fade from my memory. Early one Monday afternoon, he suddenly made his appearance in my engraving room, looking pale and haggard and with a wild expression in his eyes. I did not let him see that I had noticed it, and shaking his hand warmly, invited him to be seated, when he began: "Mr. Sartain, I have come to you for protection and refuge. It will be difficult for you to believe what I have to tell - that such things could be in the nineteenth century. It is necessary that I remain concealed for a time. Can I stay here with you?"

"Certainly," said I, "as long as you like. You will be perfectly safe here." He thanked me and then went into an explanation of what was the matter.

He said that he was on his way to New York, when he overheard some men who sat a few seats back of him plotting how they would kill him and throw him from the platform of the car. He said they spoke so low that it would have been impossible for him to hear and understand the meaning of their words, had it not been that his sense of hearing was so acute. They did not guess that he heard them, as he sat so quiet and suppressed all indication of having heard the plot.

He watched an opportunity to give them the slip at Bordentown, and when the train arrived at the station he stepped to the platform and kept out of sight till the train had moved on again. He had returned to Philadelphia by the first return conveyance and had hurried to me for shelter.

I assure him that he was perfectly welcome, but that it was my belief that the whole thing was a creation of his fancy, for what interest could these people have in taking his life, and at such risk to themselves?

He said, "It was revenge."

"Revenge for what?" said I.

He answered, "Well, a woman trouble."

I placed him comfortably, and then went on with my work, which was in a hurry. Occasionally conversation passed between us, and I observed a singular change in the current of his thoughts. He had rushed in on me in terror for his life, in fear that he might be killed, and now I perceived that he had drifted round to the idea that it would be good to kill himself.

After a long silence, he said suddenly, "If this mustache of mine were removed, I should not be so readily recognized. Will you lend me a razor, that I may shave it off?" I told him that, as I never shaved, I had no razor, but if he wanted it removed, I could do that for him almost as close with scissors. Accordingly, I took him to the bathroom and performed the operation successfully.

After tea, it being now dark, he prepared to go out, and on my asking him where he was going, he said, "To the Schuykill." I told him that I would go too, to which he offered no objection. His shoes were worn down a good deal on the outer side of the heels, and he complained that his feet were chafed in consequence, and hurt him, so I gave him my slippers to wear, as I had no second pair of shoes that would serve. When we had reached the corner of Ninth and Chestnut Streets, we waited there for an omnibus, and among other things he said was that he wished

I would see to it that after his death the painting Osgood made of him should go to his mother (meaning Mrs. Clemm). I promised him that as far as I could control it, that should be done.

We entered an omnibus and rode to its stopping place, a tavern on the north side of Callowhill Street, on the bend it takes toward the northwest to reach the Fairmount Bridge. At this place, there was light enough, chiefly from what shone out through the door of the tavern, but beyond was darkness, and forward into the darkness we went.

I kept on his left side, and on nearly approaching the bridge, I guided him off to the right by a gentle pressure until we reached the foot of the lofty flight of steep wooden steps that ascended almost to the top of the reservoir. Here was the first landing, and with seats, so we sat down. All this time I had contrived to keep him in conversation, which never ceased except when we were on our way up that breakneck flight of stairs. I had reckoned on the moon's rising, but it did not: I had forgotten that each evening it rose so much later. There we sat at that dizzy height in perfect darkness, for clouds hid the stars, and I hoping for the moon which came not.

As they say on the landing, Poe began telling Sartain about a random series of "visions" that he had experienced while being held in jail for public drunkenness. One of them was of a radiant white woman who directed a stream of questions at him. His fate, he was told, depended on his answers. Another was of a caldron of boiling liquid, presented to him with the threat that he would be "lifted by the hair of my head and dipped into the hot liquid up to my lips." The last was a horrific scene showing, to Poe's horror, Maria Clemm being dismembered.

Sartain continued:

These are examples of the kind of talk I listened to up there in the darkness; but, as everything has an end, so had this, and we descended the stairway slowly and cautiously, holding well on to the handrails. By still keeping him talking I got him back to an omnibus that waited for passengers at the tavern door, and when exactly abreast of the step I pressed against him and raised his foot to it, but instantly recollecting himself, he drew back, when I gently pushed him, saying "Go on," and having got him seated with myself beside him, said, "You were saying so and so," and he responded by continuing the subject he had been speaking on.

I took him home safe to Sansom Street, made him a bed on the sofa in the dining room, and slept alongside of him on three chairs, without undressing.

On the second morning, he seemed to have become so like his old self that I trusted him to go out alone. Regular meals and rest had a good effect; but his mind was not yet free from all nightmare. After an hour or two, he returned, then he told me that he had arrived at the conclusion that what I said was true, that the whole thing had been a delusion and a scare created out of his own excited imagination. He said that his mind began to clear as he lay on the grass, his face buried in it, and his nostrils inhaling its sweet fragrance mingled with the odor of the earth; that the words he heard kept running through his mind, but somehow, he tried in vain to connect them with who spoke them, and this his thoughts gradually awakened into rational order and he saw that he came out of a dream.

I had asked him how he came to be in Moyamensing Prison, and he said that had been suspected of trying to pass a fifty-dollar counterfeit note; but the truth is it was for what takes so many there for a few hours only, the drop too much... Being

now all right again, he was ready to go to New York.
He borrowed what was needful and departed. I never
saw him more.

It is an odd and interesting account, which contains at least one error that we know of. Poe was not on his way to New York when the incident occurred - he was on his way to Richmond. He was in Philadelphia for two weeks in July, during which time he was jailed for public intoxication but was released by a sympathetic judge, visited Sartain and told him that men were chasing him, and then visited Lippard when he ran out of money and needed train fare to continue his journey.

Sartain may have been wrong about that one part of the story, but he was right about Poe's behavior and his wild story about men who were chasing him and trying to kill him for "revenge." After leaving Sartain, Poe evidently tried to complete the disguise by buying used, secondhand clothing, which is what he was wearing when he arrived at Lippard's office.

Sartain never realized the error and repeated it when he told the story again for the *Philadelphia Record* a few years later. This version of his story is slightly different than the last.

The first instance of hallucination I ever detected
in Poe occurred about a month before his tragic
death. I was at work in my shirt-sleeves, in my
office on Sansom Street, when Poe burst in upon me
excitedly, and exclaimed, "I have come to you for
refuge." I saw at a glance that he was suffering
from some mental overstrain and assured him of
shelter. I then begged him to explain.

"I was just on my way to New York on the train,"
he said to me, "when I heard whispering going on
behind me. Owing to my marvelous power of
hearing I was enabled to overhear what the
conspirators were saying. Just imagine such a thing
in the nineteenth century! They were plotting to
murder me. I immediately left the train and

hastened back here again. I must disguise myself in some way. I must shave off this mustache at once. Will you lend me a razor?"

Afraid to trust him with it, I told him that I hadn't any, but I could remove his mustache with the scissors. Taking him to the rear of the office I sheared away until he was absolutely barefaced. This satisfied him somewhat and I managed to calm him.

That very evening, however, he prepared to leave the house. "Where are you going? I asked. "To the Schuylkill," he replied. "Then I am going with you," I declared. He did not object, and together we walked to Chestnut Street and took a bus.

A steep flight of steps used to lead up from the Schuylkill then, and ascending these we sat on a bench overlooking the stream. The night was black, without a star, and I felt somewhat nervous alone with Poe in the condition he was in. Going up in the bus he said to me," after my death see that my mother (Mrs. Clemm) gets that portrait of me from Osgood."

Now he began to talk the wildest nonsense, in the weird, dramatic style of his tales. He said he had been thrown into Moyamensing Prison for forging a check and while there, a white female form had appeared on the battlements and addressed him in whispers..."

Again, Sartain recalled Poe's hallucinations - the supposed "visions" of the woman in white and the caldron of boiling liquid, but the murder of Maria Clemm was not mentioned. The details are sparser but basically, it's the same story as before. The conclusion of the account is also the same, although with fewer details:

By and by, I suggested we descend again and Poe assented. All the way down the steep steps, I trembled lest he should remember his resolve of suicide, but I kept his mind from it and got him back safely. Three days after, he went out again and returned in the same mood. "I lay on the earth with my nose in the grass," he said then, "and the smell revived me. I began at once to realize the falsity of my hallucinations."

In Sartain's account - both versions because they are basically the same - he makes it clear that Poe arrives at his office in a manic state, believing that someone is trying to kill him. While Poe isn't quoted as saying it in either account, he also makes it clear that he is afraid that his friend is suicidal.

In the Lippard account - which I am convinced happened just before Poe left the city - no mention is made of suicide or even of Poe believing that he is being chased, but he is desperate to leave town. Lippard never mentions Poe's mustache, which might have been growing back by then, but we have to remember that he had not seen him in five years. For all he knew, Poe had been cleanshaven for a long time.

Unfortunately, we don't have an exact date for when each of the incidents occurred, but we do know when Poe was in Philadelphia, so they must have taken place during that time frame, before he traveled on to Richmond.

We do know that Poe was jailed during that time and we also know that he wrote a letter to Maria Clemm from Philadelphia on July 7. The letter seems to show him in a suicidal state of mind, brought on by his remorse over having once again fallen victim to the bottle, as well as his continued grieving for Virginia. Poe had engaged in self-destructive behavior after her death that was extreme, even for him. He was in deep despair while in Philadelphia, perhaps, I believe, descending into madness.

He wrote to Maria, "The very instant you get this, come to me. The joy of seeing you will almost compensate me for our sorrows. We can but die together. It's no use to reason with me now;

I must die. I have no desire to live since I have done 'Eureka'... For your sake it would be sweet to live, but we must die together."

Poe's inclusion of his devoted mother-in-law in his suicide-pact shows how out of touch with reality he was at that moment - just before going to Sartain's office.

Maria did not come to Philadelphia because the letter didn't reach her in New York until after the crisis had passed. After a few days with Sartain, his crushing despair had dissipated, and he wrote a follow-up letter to Maria on July 14 from the American Hotel. He was still remorseful, but he was better. His talk of suicide was over - for now.

But there is one last thing before we move on that should be addressed. If the story of the men plotting Poe's death on the train sounded familiar, it's because you've read it before. After Poe's death, Dr. Moran claimed that a train conductor named Rollins recalled Poe going north on the train, only to get off the train at the river crossing and return to Baltimore. Why? Because he claimed men were following him.

The conductor did say that he saw a couple of men who looked like "sharks" in the car, but only after Poe had made him aware of the threat. What does this mean for our investigation of Poe's last days? It means that Poe reverted back to something familiar when he began having a manic episode and believing that someone was trying to kill him.

But was he really in danger? That remains to be seen.

Over the years, there have been a number of theories to explain Poe's death, including "cooping," as we discussed earlier. Some of the theories seem plausible, while others are a little harder to swallow. Let's start with the basics:

Alcohol Poisoning

As we have discussed already, Poe had a rather odd problem when it came to alcohol. It was likely genetic because his sister had the same problem. Many of his friends noted that, on occasion, even one glass of wine could make Poe staggeringly drunk.

We do know that Poe joined the temperance society after renewing his romance with Elmira Shelton, but he had struggled with alcohol his entire life. There are claims that state that Poe was told by a doctor in Richmond that if he had another drunken spell like he'd experienced in Philadelphia, it could turn out to be fatal. I do believe that Poe had already done severe damage to his body and mind with his past blackout spells, caused by alcohol, so I suppose that means that I feel that alcohol contributed to his death, even though I don't believe it was the sole cause of it.

Others disagree with me, however. Poe's friend J.P. Kennedy wrote on October 10, 1849, "On Tuesday last, Edgar A. Poe died in town here at the hospital from the effects of a debauch. He fell in with some companion here who seduced him to the bottle, which it was said he had renounced some time ago. The consequence was fever, delirium, and madness, and in a few days a termination of his sad career in the hospital. Poor Poe! A bright but unsteady light has been awfully quenched."

Poe *could* have died from alcohol poisoning, but does this explain his five-day disappearance or his secondhand clothes?

No, but it still became a popular theory, mostly because of Joseph Snodgrass. Even though at one point Dr. Moran, the only somewhat reliable physician, claimed that Poe was *not* drunk when he arrived at the hospital, Snodgrass told a different story - and he might have had a motive for doing so. Snodgrass was one of the leading members in a national temperance society and gave lectures across the country about the evils of alcohol. He blamed Poe's death on binge drinking and there's no question that it made a frightening bit of propaganda. Modern science has thrown a bit of a wrench into Snodgrass' story, though. Samples of Poe's hair have been tested and show low levels of lead, which is an indication that Poe remained faithful to his vow of sobriety up until his death.

As I mentioned earlier, I believe that Poe's drinking spree in Philadelphia was his last. That's not to say that he didn't have a drink or two after his arrival in Richmond - and before joining the temperance society - but I don't believe he ever engaged again in one of his epic drunks.

Carbon Monoxide Poisoning

In 1999, a public health researcher named Albert Donnay claimed that Poe's death was caused from carbon monoxide poisoning from coal gas that was used for indoor lighting during that time. He also had clippings of Poe's hair tested, this time for the presence of certain heavy metals. This would have revealed the presence of coal gas. The test turned out to be inconclusive, however, so it was a good try, but ultimately not a solution.

Mercury Poisoning

This theory is a little more inventive and does check off some of the boxes about Poe's death. Donnay's test failed to find evidence of carbon monoxide, but it did find elevated levels of mercury in Poe's system. This might explain some of the hallucinations and delirium that Poe experienced before he died - but only if the levels were high.

They weren't. Most likely, the trace levels of mercury in Poe's blood came from a drug called calomel, which Poe was prescribed after his time in jail in Philadelphia. An outbreak of cholera had occurred in the city in July 1849, when Poe was there. Calomel, which the doctor prescribed, was mercury chloride, which explained the small amounts found in Poe's hair.

Rabies

Sorry, but this is a weird one. In 1996, Dr. R. Michael Benitez was participating in a clinical pathologic conference where doctors were given patients, along with a list of symptoms, and were instructed to diagnose and compare with other doctors, along with the written record. The symptoms of an anonymous patient - listed only as "a writer from Richmond" - were clear: the man had died from rabies. According to the patient's physician, he had been admitted to the hospital due to "lethargy and confusion." Once admitted, the patient began a rapid downward spiral, exhibiting delirium, visual hallucinations, wide changes in pulse rate, and rapid, shallow breathing. Within four days - the average length of survival after the onset of serious rabies symptoms, the patient was dead.

Benitez later found out that his theoretical patient was not just an average "writer from Richmond." The patient he had diagnosed was Edgar Allan Poe. Rabies was a fairly common virus in the nineteenth century, so Benitez believed he'd solved the mystery of Poe's death. He published an article about it in the September 1996 issue of the *Maryland Medical Journal*. As he pointed out in the article, without DNA evidence, it was impossible to say with certainty that Poe died from rabies, but it seemed to fit.

Well, sort of.

The biggest problem with the theory is that Poe showed no evidence of hydrophobia - a fear of water - which was a tell-tale sign of rabies. Poe drank water right up until the hour of his death. There was also no evidence of an animal bite, which is how the virus is transmitted, and no record of foaming at the mouth, another important syndrome.

Brain Tumor

One of the most recent theories about Poe's death suggests that he died from a brain tumor, which influenced his behavior before his death. When Poe died, he was buried in an unmarked grave in the Old Western Burial Grounds. More than 25 years later, a monument was erected for Poe at the entrance to the cemetery, so his body was moved. During the process, the coffin fell apart and Poe's remains were dumped on the ground. Little remained of his body, but one worker did remark on a strange feature of Poe's skull - a mass that was inside of it. Newspapers of the day claimed that the clump was Poe's brain, shriveled yet intact after all those years in the ground.

Today, we know that could not have been Poe's brain. It would have been one of the first parts of his body to decompose. But, according to a pathologist, it could have been a tumor, which could calcify after death into a hard mass. There is a claim that a doctor in New York once told Poe that he had a lesion on his brain that caused his adverse reaction to alcohol.

Was that the tumor those cemetery workers allegedly saw? No one knows. There's no evidence either way.

Influenza

It has also been theorized that Poe died from something as simple as influenza, which turned into a deadly pneumonia while he was on his deathbed. There are the rumors that Poe had visited his doctor on his last night in Richmond, who suggested that he postpone his trip, due to the fact that he wasn't feeling well. According to newspaper reports, it was raining in Baltimore when Poe was there and some believe that his own clothes were drenched, which was why he was wearing an outfit from a secondhand store. The cold and rain could have worsened the flu that he already had, eventually leading to pneumonia. A high fever might account for his hallucinations and his confusion.

The biggest flaw that I see here is that even doctors in the nineteenth century would have recognized the flu. Dr. Moran, while young, was a resident physician in a hospital. He would have been able to diagnose influenza. He also would have noted it if Poe's fever had been high enough to cause hallucinations. He didn't. His mentions of "fever" seemed to be of the mental kind, not the raising of his body temperature.

Beaten to Death

This theory is going to take some explaining - how it got started, how it developed, and how it created the theory that Poe was murdered. For this section, we have to start at the beginning, when the first theory about Poe's death that didn't involve alcohol was suggested in 1857.

The writer was Elizabeth Oakes Smith, who penned an article called "Autobiographic Notes: Edgar Allan Poe." She had first met Poe around 1845 when Elizabeth, her husband, Seba, and their four sons moved from Maine to New York to immerse themselves in the city's literary world. Both Elizabeth and Seba had already gained reputations as talented and prolific authors and every month, work from one or both of them appeared in one of the leading journals. Seba enjoyed a niche as a popular author, riding on the success of a character he'd created named Major Jack Downing, one of America's first homespun, comic commentators. In time, his wife's fame would surpass his own when she began writing novels and plays and joined the lecture circuit.

The Smiths crossed paths with Poe many times over the next four years, meeting casually in the homes of mutual friends or at literary gatherings. Poe, not surprisingly, had printed some harsh things about some

One of Poe's greatest posthumous defenders, author Elizabeth Oakes Smith

of Elizabeth's work, notably a long poem she published called *The Sinless Child*. He found it full of flaws, but still conceded that it had great merit. Poe wrote, "She has very narrowly missed one of those happy creations which now and then immortalize the poet." It was one of those comments that Poe was so good at, leaving the target of his criticism confused as to whether be happy or resentful.

Seba Smith fared far worse. Poe had been rough with his feelings about Smith's poem *Powhatan*, published in 1841, in *Graham's Magazine*. He called it "absurdly flat," and a work with "so grotesque an air of bombast and assumption," among other things. But Elizabeth wrote that she and her husband harbored no ill will against Poe. He was simply doing his job. Poe the critic "did not play with his pen," she later said, "but wielded it. Right or wrong, all was real at the time. He was terribly in earnest."

For Poe, it was good that she felt that way because soon after his death, she became one of his greatest defenders. Over the next 20 years, as Poe's reputation was undergoing a fierce posthumous attack, Elizabeth wrote three different articles trying to explain his spirit to a fascinated public. In each of them, she made reference to the manner of his death. What she had to say was both unexpected and shocking.

In the 1857 article, which appeared in *United States Magazine*, she wrote an informed discussion of his life and career, and added this:

> *Not long before his death he was cruelly beaten, blow upon blow, by a ruffian who knew of no better mode of avenging supposed injuries. It is well known that a brain fever followed - that he left New York precipitately - that he reached Baltimore, the city of his nativity, and there died on the 4th of October 1849.*
>
> *The hand should be palsied, and the name blighted, of the man who, under any provocation, could inflict a blow on a slender, helpless, intellectual being, however misguided, like Edgar A. Poe.*

There is confusion in her statement, of course - she missed the date of Poe's death and made an error about where his journey started, among other things. Poe was hardly a "helpless" intellectual. In his youth, he had been an athlete, had served in the army, and in past skirmishes had proven to be far from helpless. Even so, it was a surprising statement for people to read. No one had considered the idea that Poe had been assaulted at this point. They only knew that he had either gone insane or, more likely, drank himself to death.

In the decade that followed Elizabeth Smith continued writing, publishing popular dime novels, children's books, and even some theatrical plays. In February 1867, she wrote again about Poe, this time in *Beadle's Monthly*. The second article was longer than the first and offered a still stronger defense of his character. Toward the end of it, she again mentions the manner of his dying, with one slight addition:

> *It is asserted in the* American Cyclopedia *that Edgar Poe died in consequence of a drunken debauch in his native city. This is not true. At the instigation*

of a woman, who considered herself injured by him, he was cruelly beaten, blow upon blow, by a ruffian who knew no better method of avenging supposed injuries. It is well known that a brain fever followed; his friends hurried him away, and he reached his native city only to breathe his last.

Once again, Mrs. Smith errs as to how Poe got to Baltimore, but interestingly, she has added that the beating that Poe supposedly suffered was because of a woman who "considered herself injured by him." This implies that it had something to do with a romantic affair.

Finally, in the *New York Home Journal* for March 15, 1876, Elizbeth put the most complete version of her beating theory into the record. It offers more details but, even so, is filled with gaps. She begins by making the distinction between a confirmed alcoholic, who never misses a day's drink, and an occasional binge drinker, a distinction that many Poe biographers have since made. She again denies, though, that drink was Poe's cause of death:

That Edgar Poe may have subjected himself to the imputation of inebriety may perhaps be conceded, or a glass of wine would act fearfully upon his delicate organization; but that he was a debauched man in any way is utterly false. He was not a diseased man from his cups at the time of his death, nor did he die from delirium tremens, as has been asserted.

The whole sad story will probably never be known, but he had corresponded freely with a woman whose name I withhold, and they having subsequently quarreled, he refused to return her letters, nor did she receive them until Dr. Griswold gave them back after Poe's death. This retention not only alarmed but exasperated the woman, and she sent an emissary of her own to enforce the delivery, and who, failing of success, beat the unhappy man in a most ruffianly manner.

A brain fever supervened, and a few friends went with him to Baltimore, his native city, which he barely reached when he died.

This final article offered more tantalizing clues, more errors, and more hints, and even though Elizabeth Smith lived until 1893, she never wrote another word about Poe's death, never named the source who provided her with information, and never offered a clue about the name of the wronged woman that she had chosen to withhold.

The beating theory was ignored for many years, likely because of the other errors in Mrs. Smith's articles and the fact that she declined to offer any real evidence that it occurred. It seemed hard to believe that Poe was beaten to death when, according to the woman who introduced the theory, she had no idea where he was coming from when he went to Baltimore or that he was in the city alone.

The only other writer who mentioned it as a possibility was Eugene Didier, who stated in 1872 that Poe, while in Baltimore, ran into some old friends from West Point, who asked him to join them for drinks. Poe, unable to handle liquor, became madly drunk from a single glass of champagne and left his friends to wander the streets. In his drunken state, he "was robbed and beaten by ruffians, and left insensible in the street all night." Once again, Didier offers no evidence for any of this. There had been no mention of "friends from West Point" in anything reported on Poe's last days, which begs the question of where this information came from.

There is also another, more important issue and it's one that Mrs. Smith hadn't dealt with either - there was no evidence that Poe had been beaten. Neither Dr. Moran nor Joseph Snodgrass - men who we know where in his presence - ever mentioned that Poe appeared to have been beaten. They never mentioned marks, cuts, scrapes, bruises, or any other signs of violence.

The first person to question the story of Poe being beaten was his old friend and former flame, Sarah Helen Whitman. It is certain that Sarah read all three of Elizabeth Smith's articles. The two women were personal friends, brought together by their shared interest in the Spiritualist movement. They kept each other informed of their writings, carried on a regular correspondence, and even vacationed together.

The first of the three articles was followed by a letter of comment from Sarah that appeared in the magazine's next issue. In it, she remarked on Poe's supposedly divided or dual nature, and added that she believed that Mrs. Smith's article would help to rid her dead friend's reputation of "some undeserved imputations." But regarding the brutal manner of death as it was described in the article, she offered no comment. She didn't comment on it after the second article either. It was after the third article, however, that she finally disputed the theory.

Another of the women that Poe almost married after Virginia's death, Sarah Helen Whitman.

Within days of its publication, she had read it and had become troubled by it, especially after the newspapers embraced the beating theory and highlighted it as something "new." Finally, sparked by a brief paragraph reprinted in several newspapers, she wrote a letter to Poe's biographer, John Ingram, and quoted the paragraph, which she found both alarming and distasteful, and offered some disturbed opinions of her own:

> *I wonder if you have heard about a scandalous paragraph which is going the rounds of the press? This is the paragraph:*
>
> *Elizabeth Oakes Smith writes in the Home Journal that the immediate cause of Edgar A. Poe's death was a severe beating which he received from the*

friend of a woman whom he had deceived and betrayed.

I have several letters denouncing Mrs. Smith for this scandalous story. Now, I do not believe that Mrs. Smith ever wrote such a paragraph or would authorize its insertion in any paper.
Some of the tribe of secret slanderers who are forever lying in wait for an occasion to sully his memory and obscure his fame have doubtless seized upon an idle and absurd story told by Mrs. S in that article which she wrote long ago for one of her own magazines, and which (as I think I told you in my last letter) she has lately republished in the Home Journal.
If you have a copy of that article you will see that her account of the cause of Poe's death has been misrepresented and misquoted, and doubtless with malign intent, by some of Poe's enemies. If I knew her present address, I would write to her at once to confirm or deny this story, which is being so widely circulated under her name.

I'm not sure what to think of this letter to Ingram. Sarah denies the story and refuses to cast blame on her friend - even though it's pretty clear that the paragraph quoted in the papers accurately portrayed what she said in her article.

Regardless, Sarah did find Elizabeth's current address and wrote to her. In her letter, she expressed a firm belief that the offensive paragraph had not come from Mrs. Smith.

But she was wrong about that. Mrs. Smith replied, and her card of explanation was included in a letter that Sarah sent to Ingram. He responded to Sarah, using the name "Eva," a nickname that Elizabeth Smith used. He wrote to Sarah Whitman:

I regret to say that I do not believe a single word of your imaginative friend Eva's denial of the paragraph in the Home Journal. I had the MS. in my hands, in her writing, containing it! Pray be careful about accepting her denial in print. I will return her card in my next.

In other words, yes, Elizabeth Smith had written the paragraph - the newspapers were quoting her accurately, no matter what she told Sarah. Elizabeth had lied to her and Sarah was shocked. More letters were exchanged with John Ingram, clarifying the statements and Sarah did her best to explain that the idea that Poe had been beaten to death because he had "betrayed and ruined" a woman were untrue.

Ingram didn't use the theory in his book and, for the most part, the idea that Poe had been murdered faded away until around 2000, when author John Evangelist Walsh revived the idea for his book about Poe's death.

He believed that Poe was beaten and murdered by the brothers of his wealthy fiancé, Elmira Shelton. Using evidence from newspapers and letters, he argued that Poe left Baltimore and made it to Philadelphia, where he was confronted by Elmira's brothers, who warned Poe against marrying their sister. Frightened by the confrontation, Poe disguised himself and hid in Philadelphia for a week before going back to Baltimore. Elmira's brothers found him there, however, beat him, and forced him to drink whiskey, which they knew would kill him.

It is an interesting take on the theory, but it does have some problems, even if we leave out the lack of any evidence that Poe had been beaten. The most problematic is that this theory proposes that the two incidents with old friends in Philadelphia - when Poe appeared in old clothing and looking for money - happened in late September 1849, not in the summer. The problem is that both men stated that the incidents occurred in the summer and we know that Poe was locked up in Philadelphia in late June for public intoxication. There is mention of him being in jail in one of the statements.

There is also no clear explanation as to why Poe would have gone to Philadelphia from Baltimore and then returned to Baltimore. He had business to attend to in Philadelphia -- which would be paying him the tidy sum of $100 - and he was on his way to New York to settle a few matters and to bring Maria Clemm back with him to Richmond.

The other problem is that this theory is also linked to Mrs. Smith's beating theory, which suggested that Poe was beaten by men who were looking for letters from a woman he had "betrayed and ruined." The book suggests that what Mrs. Smith was talking about was the situation with Elmira and her brothers.

But this makes no sense. Elmira Shelton had no problems with Poe and there were no letters. When Poe left on his trip, they were engaged to be married and planned to hold the ceremony after he returned from his trip. It's certainly possible that Elmira's brothers were not thrilled with their sister's choice in a prospective husband - we know that her children were not - but there's no evidence to say that they followed Poe to Philadelphia, or even to Baltimore.

When it comes to letters and death threats, the only scandal connected to Poe that might have put his life in danger was what happened between Poe, the poet Elizabeth Ellet, and Fanny Osgood, with whom Poe had engaged in an affair and with whom he'd allegedly had a daughter.

Accounts of the particulars of the scandal and the sequence of events differ, but at the time, Poe was at the height of his fame after the publication of "The Raven." A number of women sent him letters, including Ellet and Osgood, and many of those letters were flirtatious or even outright sexual. Ellet possibly believed that she was in competition with Fanny, who Poe had written several poems about around this time.

During a visit to Poe's home in January 1846, Elizabeth Ellet allegedly saw letters from Fanny, shown to her by Poe's wife, Virginia, and she subsequently advised Fanny to ask for their return, implying to Fanny that the letters were indiscreet. On Fanny's behalf, two friends, Margaret Fuller and Anne Lynch Botta, asked Poe to return her letters. Poe was angry at their interference, which he blamed on Ellet. He suggested to Elizabeth that she had "better look after her own letters," which were just as indiscreet. He then gathered up the letters from Elizabeth and left them at her house.

But apparently, those weren't all the letters that she had sent to Poe. Elizabeth asked her brother, Colonel William Lummis, to get the rest of the letters from him. He first challenged Poe to a duel, which Poe refused, and then threatened to kill him if he encountered him on the street. Poe was so concerned about the threat that he borrowed a pistol from Thomas Dunn English, which he kept for the remainder of his life.

Meanwhile, Elizabeth was threatened with legal action if she didn't stop claiming that Poe and Fanny were having an affair -- even though they were. She formally apologized and retracted her statements, claiming that the letter that Virginia had shown her "must have forgery created by Poe himself." She blamed the entire incident on Poe, suggesting that he was "intemperate and subject to acts of lunacy." The rumor that Poe was insane was spread by Ellet and other enemies of Poe and was eventually reported in the newspapers.

Virginia was deeply affected by the scandal. For nearly a year, she had been receiving anonymous letters, probably from Ellet, which reported her husband's alleged indiscretions. On her deathbed, Virginia was even said to have claimed, "Mrs. E. had been her murderer."

As Poe described it, "I scorned Mrs. E. simply because she revolted me, and to this day she has never ceased her anonymous persecutions."

He would remember the incident - and the threats from William Lummis - until the day he died.

Another Possible Theory

I don't think that we will ever know exactly what happened to Edgar Allan Poe in the days that led up to his death. We'll never know the cause of his death either. It could have been one thing, or perhaps a combination of things.

If he did die from "brain fever," or what's better known as phrenitis, an inflammation of the brain that includes acute fever and delirium, then it's possible there was an underlying cause like encephalitis or meningitis.

But what finally pushed Poe over the edge? Was it a physical ailment, a mental one, or - as I believe - a combination of both?

As I have stated already, I am no Poe scholar. But I am fascinated by the man, by his life, his afterlife, and most of all, by his mysterious death. I have spent years pondering what led to Poe's disappearance and how he ended up being found at Ryan's Tavern that day. I don't claim to have all the answers, but I do have a theory to suggest. It not only includes some parts of other theories, but I believe it answers some questions that some of the other theories don't. You will, of course, have to decide what you think of it for yourself.

I'd like to start my story by going back to June 1849, when Poe arrived in Philadelphia while on his trip to Richmond. He was, without doubt, a wreck at this point in his life. Six months earlier, while still in mourning over Virginia's death, he had been engaged in an erratic pursuit of several women, including one that he'd asked to marry him. He had even attempted suicide - or at least pretended to - back in November. Worst of all, he was drinking heavily, even though doctors had told him that if he continued to do so, it could be fatal.

In late June, when he arrived in Philadelphia, he went on one of his infamous binges and was arrested for public drunkenness. While in Moyamensing, he suffered a terrifying alcoholic withdrawal, complete with hallucinations and seizures.

I believe this final binge seriously affected Poe's mental health, which had already been teetering toward a break with reality. Months of depression and anxiety - mental states Poe had long been familiar with - led to a near breakdown after he introduced alcohol into his system once again.

As we have discussed several times, Poe had a strange reaction to alcohol as well as to other drugs, like laudanum, which was opium-based. I tend to believe that this was likely caused by his brain chemistry, which was possibly the source of his depression and melancholy. Doctors knew little about the human brain in those days and Poe could not have been diagnosed with any kind of mental Illness during a time when physicians had no idea what those illnesses were. Instead, they called them things like "brain fever" or simply "insanity." As psychiatric diagnoses improved, those same issues began to be called clinical depression, acute anxiety, manic depression, and bipolar disorder.

When Poe started drinking in Philadelphia, it led to his arrest. Once he sobered up behind bars, a sympathetic judge released him. Poe was no longer under the influence of alcohol, but he was under the influence of his mental illness, which the alcohol had exacerbated.

It was at this point that Poe went to visit his friend Sartain, who spoke of Poe's erratic behavior and his fear that someone was looking for him. This led to his disguise, his secondhand clothing, and even shaving off his mustache to hide his identity. This was textbook manic behavior. I believe that, in Poe's mind, he was hiding from Colonel William Lummis, Elizabeth Ellet's brother, who had sworn to kill him. Was he still looking for Poe, trying to enact his revenge? Most likely he wasn't, but to Poe, in his weakened mental state, the threat was very current and very real.

Poe made it out of the city, arrived in Richmond rather the worse for wear, and spent a few days recuperating at his hotel before visiting family and friends and finally, becoming reacquainted with Elmira Shelton. By then, Poe was no longer manic and was back to being himself.

But it wouldn't last.

Poe was already acting strangely before he left Richmond. He began complaining of not feeling well, talked of postponing his trip, and even visited a doctor. He was last seen having supper and then walking down to the river to meet the boat that would take him to Baltimore. Why not return to his hotel and rest before he traveled? Because Poe was already becoming manic again. His manic-depressive cycle had him on the upswing and he was too restless to sleep.

It would have only taken a little alcohol to again send Poe off into the same kind of state that he was in when he was in Philadelphia. In fact, according to Joseph Snodgrass, that's exactly what killed him. But what about the reports from Dr. Moran that Poe *wasn't* drunk when he was brought to the hospital?

It's always assumed that Poe drank himself to death because he was found in a gutter outside of Ryan's Tavern, but keep in mind, a "tavern" wasn't necessarily a saloon in those days. It was more like an inn, and while Ryan's did serve liquor, it was also a respectable polling place. This was not a cheap and seedy dive on the harbor.

And, as it turned out, Snodgrass turned out to be a rather unreliable witness after it was discovered that he was a leader in the American temperance and used Poe as an example of how liquor could "ruin a man's life."

But since there is no evidence that Poe was beaten and no evidence that he was drunk, then what could have put him in the kind of condition that he ended up in?

Before he was found, Poe repeated his behavior from Philadelphia. Initially, he boarded the northbound train but, as he become more manic, he started to believe that men were following him, perhaps even William Lummis. When the train stopped at the river crossing, he got back on board and returned to Baltimore, believing that he could blend into the city and escape.

When he made it back, Poe again sought out a disguise. He left his case, his papers, and his extra clothing in storage at a hotel and found a place to buy secondhand clothing that he could wear as a disguise. Why not stay in hiding at the hotel? He was too manic to lock himself in a small room by the train station. Perhaps believing he would be discovered there, it seemed safest on the streets. But as his mania increased, he lost track of time and his surroundings and ended up "hiding" in the city for days before he was discovered by Walker in front of Ryan's Tavern.

But, if not alcohol, then what triggered Poe's break with reality?

I believe - and I'm theorizing here -- that Poe's serious manic episodes were caused by outside influences, usually alcohol. But if Poe wasn't drunk, and hadn't been drinking in Baltimore, then it had to be something else. Even though Poe was found in secondhand clothing, a disguise as a down-and-out working man would not have been so complete that he would have had no money in his pockets. We do know that the usually broke Poe actually had a little money for a change. He'd recently earned some and undoubtedly, he would have had some on his trip. When he was found, though, his pockets were empty. This leads me to think that Poe was the victim of a robbery. Remember that Poe was always nicely dressed and took care of his clothing. With his well-brushed suit and walking stick, he would have made an attractive target to a would-be thief or ruffian.

But this was no ordinary street mugging. I think Poe went into the wrong place to have a meal when he first arrived in Baltimore. Before he first boarded the train to leave the city, before he returned, before he left his belongings in storage at the hotel, before he acquired secondhand clothing as a disguise, and certainly before his mind snapped, Poe went into a restaurant to eat.

He didn't buy alcohol to wash down his food, though. There was no need. His food or his drink had an ingredient that didn't belong there and which, I believe, pushed Poe over the edge.

Someone slipped him what would eventually become known as a "Mickey Finn."

Of course, that moniker wouldn't be attached to what was commonly known as "knock out drops" until more than 50 years after Poe's death, but a substance like chloral hydrate had been used to prey on the vulnerable for many years before Poe walked into a tavern in Baltimore to get a bite to eat before he left on the train.

Mixtures, powders, and potions that caused people to lose consciousness and not remember what happened to them started to be called a "Mickey Finn" thanks to a real person of that name who ran a notorious Chicago saloon in the city's Levee vice district. Finn opened his dive - the Lone Star Saloon and Palm Garden, which had a single potted palm tree in the "garden" - in 1896. In addition to a drinking establishment, Finn also fenced stolen goods, supervised pickpockets, and offered rooms to prostitutes.

At some point, Finn obtained a supply of some kind of white powder that may have been chloral hydrate. He made it the key ingredient of two knockout drinks -- the "Mickey Finn Special," consisting of raw alcohol, water in which snuff had been soaked, and a dollop of white stuff; and "Number Two," beer mixed with a jolt of white powder plus the aforementioned snuff water.

Patrons who tried either of these powders lost control of their behavior, were stripped of their valuables, and usually dumped in the alley. They woke the next morning with little memory of the night before.

Finn evidently paid off the cops but became such a nuisance -- even by Chicago standards -- that his bar was shut down in 1903. He was never prosecuted, though, and after a brief hiatus returned to bartending, having sold his special recipes to other tavern owners. Eventually "Mickey Finn" became the name for any sort of knockout punch.

And I want you to take note of one more Chicago story that I believe adds to the theory that this might have happened to Poe in October 1849.

Years later, in 1918, the staff and the owners of various restaurants downtown were arrested due to the apparent widespread practice of poisoning their guests. Patrons who tipped poorly were slipped a concoction through their food and drinks that contained antimony potassium tartrate.

Exposure to the drug - which is still used as a diaphoretic or expectorant in certain cough syrups - could cause headaches, dizziness, vomiting, and memory loss, and could be lethal in large quantities. Because it was used to treat parasitical infections in the nineteenth century, it was fairly easy to come by.

In the Chicago case, W. Stuart Wood and his wife were arrested for manufacturing the knockout powder and two bartenders were arrested for selling the powder at the bar in the waiter's union headquarters. The packets of powder - named after Mickey Finn - were sold for 20-cents.

How does this connect to Poe? If Poe was slipped some kind of knockout powder in the establishment he visited, it would explain his behavior during the next few days.

After leaving the tavern, he went to the train station and boarded his train. During the journey, he became more confused and more paranoid. The drugs didn't cause Poe to become unconscious - not yet anyway, we don't know what occurred during his missing days - but the paranoia that he suffered in Philadelphia returned and he convinced himself that he was being followed.

And it's possible that he was - perhaps the men on the train really were following Poe, planning to rob him of his money. They could have been men from the tavern where he was dosed. Perhaps they followed him back to Baltimore - or perhaps Poe imagined the pursuit, we'll never know.

What we do know is that Poe returned to Baltimore, stashed his belongings at the hotel near the train station, at some point traded his suit for secondhand clothing that I believe was meant to be a disguise, and vanished into the back alleys of Baltimore for several days. The poison had seeped into his system by now, but in so doing, had triggered a return of his past mania, perhaps made worse by drugs that caused nausea, vomiting, hallucinations, and memory loss.

By the time that Walker found him in that gutter in front of Ryan's Tavern, he was lucky that Poe remembered who he was, let alone the name of Joseph Snodgrass.

Poe never really regained consciousness - or sanity - while in the hospital. He continued to call for someone named "Reynolds," but we will never know who that was. He finally died, a mixture of the mental illness that had long plagued him and the drugs that he'd ingested into his system that finally proved fatal. Dr. Moran called it "brain fever" and maybe that's as good a name for it as any other.

Needless to say, I can't offer any proof that this is what caused Poe to go missing for several days and eventually killed him, but I think it's as plausible a theory as many others -- and even more so than most.

The death of the "Raven" will always be a mystery. It's never going to be solved and, honestly, I don't think Edgar Allan Poe would want it another way.

9. Secrets of the Grave

THERE ARE SOME SECRETS WHICH DO NOT PERMIT THEMSELVES TO BE TOLD.
— EDGAR ALLAN POE

The cemetery where Poe was buried in Baltimore is one of the most compelling graveyards in America, although many people are unaware that a large part of it even exists. It is called the Old Western - or Westminster - Burial Grounds and it holds the remains of several famous politicians, military generals, and a writer - Edgar Allan Poe.

The legends say that Poe's ghost walks here, along with the spirits of others buried in the graveyard, but if he does, that's not even the strangest mystery connected to this place.

Earlier, we described the sad and rather forlorn occasion of Poe's burial in the cemetery in 1849. As years passed and Poe's reputation grew, the force of his personality overshadowed anyone else who was buried on the grounds. People came searching for his burial site, only to find it unmarked and largely forgotten.

Eventually, the sexton, George W. Spence, placed a small block of sandstone on the grave and marked it with the number

"80." But this wasn't enough for those who idolized the man who created "The Raven" and so many tales of the macabre. Reports of his anonymous, overgrown, and unkempt grave began to circulate, first privately and then in the newspapers.

In 1860, Maria Clemm wrote to Neilson Poe from Alexandria, Virginia, "A lady called on me a short time ago from Baltimore. She said she had visited my darling Eddie's grave. She said it was in the basement of the church, covered with rubbish and coal. Is this true? Please let me know. I am certain both he and I have still friends left to rescue his loved remains from degradation."

If the "basement of the church" comment sounds odd to you, we'll come back to that, although Poe's grave was never in that spot.

It was, however, still unmarked and this note of concern from Maria seems to have spurred Neilson to action. He assured Maria that Poe was buried in the family plot, but he did tell her that he would make sure that the grave was better maintained. Soon after, he ordered a marble headstone for his cousin's burial site. It was in the process of being carved by Hugh Sisson at his shop, which was next to the railroad yard. Because of the weight of the stones and the difficulty of moving them, this was a prime location for a stone carver.

Until it wasn't, that is.

Before the stone could be installed at the cemetery, a train derailed in the yard and crashed into Sisson's shop. The stone was destroyed in the accident and Neilson couldn't afford to buy another one. Poe's grave remained unmarked until after the Civil War.

In 1865, a movement was underway, started by Miss Sara Sigourney Rice, to provide a monument for Poe. Through a combination of pennies collected by teachers and students, gifts from friends, and a variety of benefits, half of the funds needed for the new monument was raised by 1871. To this day, visitors to Poe's grave can still find pennies that have been left behind. They are a tribute to the hard work of Miss Rice and the students who collected the money to create the monument - one penny at a time.

The remainder of the money required was donated by Mr. George W. Childs of Philadelphia in 1874. Designed by George A. Frederick - who was the architect for Baltimore's City Hall - and

The final resting place of Poe and his family at the Westminster Burial Ground in Baltimore. The monument was paid for by students from all over the country who raised money for it one penny at a time.

carved by Hugh Sisson, work soon began on the monument. This time, only one accident occurred as Sisson worked -- Poe's birthday is erroneously given as January 20 rather than January 19.

After discussion on the most appropriate place for the imposing stone, it was decided that it would be best seen in the front corner of the cemetery. In 1852, a church had been built on the site and it would have blocked the view of Poe's stone if it had been left in his grandfather's plot. There was also a problem with securing rights to the surrounding property, most of which was already occupied.

The monument was dedicated on November 17, 1875, and among those in attendance were John H.B. Latrobe - one of the judges who awarded Poe with the *Baltimore Saturday Visitor* prize in 1833 - Neilson Poe, and Walt Whitman, the great American poet who had once met Poe. Letters were read from Henry Longfellow, John G. Whittier, William Cullen Bryant, and Alfred Tennyson.

Poe's body had to be exhumed and moved to the new burial site at the front of the cemetery. Because he had been buried in a cheap wooden coffin, it came as no surprise that it broke apart during the move and what remained of Poe's body fell onto the ground. George W. Spence, the same sexton who buried Poe in 1849, supervised the reburial in a new coffin.

Pieces of the original coffin are now collector's items and can still be purchased for a steep price. Rumor has it that one of Poe's many female admirers wore a cross fashioned from pieces of the coffin wood for many years. His fans of the 1870s were truly America's first "goths."

Maria Clemm was also buried at the site with Poe when she passed away in 1855 - and oddly, so was Virginia.

Virginia had died before Poe did and she was originally interred in their landlord's family crypt in the Bronx. After Poe was moved to the new monument, some of his admirers decided that Virginia needed to be moved to Baltimore to lay next to her husband. The problem was that developers had already built over the cemetery in the Bronx where she had been entombed and had moved the bodies. Fortunately, though, one of Poe's early biographers, the eccentric William Gill, had rescued Virginia's bones. But unfortunately, he had taken her remains home with him and forgot where he'd put them for years. Eventually, he found them - they were in a box under his bed - and he sent them to Baltimore for reburial. Virginia's body was placed next to the monument on the south side, close to both Poe and her mother. The three who had struggled together as a family for so many years were now together for eternity.

But that's not quite the end of the story of Poe's grave - he is the only person buried in the cemetery who has two gravestones.

In 1913, Orrin C. Painter, a prominent businessman and philanthropist with a deep interest in Poe, placed another stone in the cemetery. It was intended to mark Poe's original burial site, but for some reason, it was misplaced against a wall rather than in the family lot. In 1921, it was moved to a more reasonable, but still

Poe's second gravestone was meant to mark his original burial site when it was installed in the cemetery in 1913. However, it was placed in the wrong spot and was moved eight years later. It's unclear today if it's in the right spot.

dubious, location. Thanks in part to this confusion - and the fact that people just love a good mystery - a rumor has persisted that the memorial committee failed to exhume Poe's remains, instead moving those of some other poor occupant of the cemetery.

Could this be true? Probably not. The 1875 exhumation was supervised by George W. Spence, who'd buried Poe in the first place. Neilson Poe was also present on both occasions. In the 25 years between Poe's death and the exhumation, both men had been frequently asked to take visitors to see Poe's grave and were unlikely to have forgotten the correct spot.

Now, what about the ghost stories of the cemetery? Is it true that Poe's ghost has been said to walk here? I can't say for sure if the stories are true, but I can assure the reader that there have been many reports of people who claim to see Poe's ghost walking through the old burial ground in the darkness - and in the daytime, as well.

The nighttime accounts are basically what you would expect - a shadowy figure in a black coat that walks through the gravestones and vanishes. Since Poe is the best-known occupant of the cemetery, most assume that it must be his restless spirit. There are a variety of reasons why he might still be restless after all these years, ranging from the mystery of his death to the unfinished business of his short life. Those who believe that someone else's body was moved to be placed under the new monument - leaving Poe's remains lost - claim that his ghost is looking for the spot where his body actually rests.

There are also a handful of reports of seeing Poe's ghost here during the daylight hours. They are as eerie - perhaps more so - than the stories that describe a figure in the darkness. In each case, witnesses have described a man wearing a black overcoat, with dark, tousled hair, and a dark mustache. One witness said that she assumed there was a Poe impersonator in the cemetery that day - that was how much the man resembled Poe. When she asked one of the staff members who sometimes conduct tours of the cemetery about the actor, she was told there was no one like the person she described at the burial ground that day.

Whoever the man was - and we assume it was the apparition of Poe - he vanished from the cemetery. When the witness and the staff member went to look for him, the enclosed cemetery was empty. No one had walked by them, which was the only path that led out of the walled cemetery to the street.

Ghost of Edgar Allan Poe aside, the cemetery itself is an odd and compelling place. The church that serves as a landmark for the graveyard was not originally on the site. The cemetery came first. It was established in 1787. The Westminster Presbyterian Church was built over a portion of it in 1852.

The cemetery, a scattering of gravestones and crumbling tombs, was effectively divided and now a large section of it can be found in the catacombs beneath the former church, now called Westminster Hall. It is a dark and foreboding place, filled with fine dust and long shadows. Tombstones still stand among the crypts and mausoleums here and sharp corners lead to recessed chambers and pits that are accessible only by ladder.

Visitors to the subterranean graveyard are not surprised to learn that a rash of suicides occurred in the catacombs between 1890 and 1920 - or that the place is allegedly haunted.

There are several ghosts said to be lingering in the catacombs - none of them Poe - and there is a legend that says the catacombs are also home to the "Screaming Skull of Cambridge."

When the church was constructed in 1852, it was built over a portion of the cemetery, which makes it seem as though it's underground. It has been dubbed the "catacombs" over the years and is regarded as one of the most haunted places in Baltimore.

The story goes that the decapitated head of a minister became haunted and that screaming sounds could be heard coming from it all hours of the day and night. The screams were said to be so terrible that they reverberated in the minds of those exposed to them for too long and several people were driven to insanity and locked away in an asylum after prolonged exposure to the skull. Eventually, some believe, the skull was brought to the catacombs beneath the church and encased in concrete to block out the sounds of the screams.

There is also the ghost of Lucia Watson Taylor, who died in Baltimore in 1816 at the age of only 16. Her spirit is said to appear as a misty figure in white who kneels in prayer at her own grave.

Another resident spirit is a woman named Leona Wellesley, a local woman who died under terrible conditions at a lunatic asylum in the city. When she died, the legends say, she was brought to the cemetery directly from the asylum, still bound in a straitjacket. She was buried under the church and forgotten - until the laughter began. The stories still say that her presence has been known to follow visitors who come to the catacombs and is sometimes heard echoing off the brick walls and emerging from the darkest corners of the chamber.

Soon after the church was completed in the early 1850s, the catacombs began to be visited by grave

The ghosts of Lucia Watson Taylor and Leona Wellesley are two of the spirits believed to linger in the catacombs beneath the church. Lucia's phantom is sometimes spotted kneeling in front of her tombstone.

robbers. They weren't looking for jewelry and valuables buried with the corpses - they were looking for the corpses themselves. Located near the cemetery at the time was Davidge Hall - the College of Medicine of Maryland - and students, unable to obtain fresh cadavers for dissection in other ways, began stealing bodies from the cemetery for their experiments to advance medical science. The catacombs, sheltered from prying eyes, became a prime target for the "resurrectionists."

But things didn't always go smoothly. On one occasion, two students from Davidge Hall were caught in the act of stealing corpses, causing a commotion among city residents. A mob was formed and chased the two young men as they made their escape. Legend has it that one of the men was captured and hanged from a nearby streetlight. Not surprisingly, his ghost is believed to haunt the catacombs, too.

If he does, he has company. Some of the lingering ghosts that still walk here are said to be those of the bodies that were removed for experimentation at the medical school. They are confused and restless, wondering where their remains have gone.

The catacombs have been frequently visited by ghost enthusiasts over the years and there are many reports of encounters with the resident spirits.

Legends also persist that some spirits here are seeking revenge on those who accidentally buried them alive. In years past, some diseases mimicked the state of death and, assuming the patients had passed away, doctors ordered them to be taken to the cemetery. Little did they know that some of those patients were still alive.

Ghost hunters have been prowling around the catacombs since as far back as August 1976, when 10 ghost hunters entered the catacombs to search for the spirit of a little girl who had been repeatedly encountered by staff members. They never saw her but could not explain the eerie footsteps that seemed to follow them throughout the graves.

Over the years, I have visited the old burial grounds - and the creepy catacombs - many times. While I have had no supernatural encounters while roaming the place, others cannot say the same. I have personally spoken to many people who have felt cold spots, heard whispers and voices, and even claim to have been touched by unseen hands. One visit to the catacombs will quickly convince you why so many people believe it to be one of the most haunted places in Baltimore.

But believe it or not, there is one more mystery connected to Poe and the old burial grounds that is even more of a mystery than lingering spirits.

This unsolved puzzle involves a mysterious figure who lurks in the cemetery one night each year but he's not a ghost - he's even stranger.

He has appeared in the graveyard for at least 70 years, and he is always described the same way. Dressed completely in black, including a black fedora and a black scarf to hide his face, he carries a walking stick and strolls into the cemetery every year in the early morning hours of January 19, the birth date of Edgar Allan

Poe. On every occasion, he has left behind a bottle of cognac and three red roses on the gravesite of the late author. After placing these items with care, he then stands, tips his hat, and walks away. The offerings always remain on the grave, although one year, they were accompanied by a note, bearing no signature, which read: "Edgar, I haven't forgotten you."

Scholars and curiosity-seekers have been baffled by the odd ritual he carries out and the significance of the items he leaves behind. The roses and cognac have been brought to the cemetery every January since 1949 and yet no clue has been offered as to the origin or true meaning of the offerings.

An infrared photograph of the original "Poe Toaster" that was taken by a *LIFE* magazine photographer July 1990.

The identity of the man has been an intriguing mystery for years. Many people, including Jeff Jerome, the curator of the nearby Edgar Allan Poe house, believe that there may be more than one person leaving the tributes. Jerome himself has seen a white-haired man while other observers have reported a man with black hair. Possibly, the second person may be the son of the man who originated the ritual. In 1993, the original visitor left a cryptic note saying, "The torch will be passed." A later note said the man, who apparently died in 1998, had handed the tradition on to his sons.

Regardless, Jerome has been quoted as saying that if he has his way, the man's identity will never be known. This is something that most Baltimore residents agree with. Jerome has received numerous telephone calls from people requesting that no attempt ever be made to approach the man.

For some time, rumors persisted that Jerome himself was the mysterious man in black, so in 1983, he invited 70 people to gather at the graveyard at midnight on January 18. They had a celebration in honor of the author's birthday with a glass of amontillado, a Spanish sherry featured in one of Poe's horror tales, and readings from the author's works. At about an hour past midnight, the celebrants were startled to see a man run through the cemetery in a black frock coat. He was fair-haired and carrying a walking stick and quickly disappeared around the cemetery's east wall. The roses and cognac were found on Poe's grave as usual.

Not to solve the mystery, but merely to enhance it, Jerome once allowed a photographer to try and capture the elusive man on film. The photographer was backed by LIFE Magazine and was equipped with rented infrared night-vision photo equipment. A radio signal triggered the camera so that the photographer could remain out of sight. The picture appeared in the July 1990 issue of LIFE and showed the back of a heavyset man kneeling at Poe's grave. His face couldn't be seen because it was shadowed by his black hat. No one else has ever been able to photograph the mysterious man again.

But in 2006, someone tried to catch him. A group of onlookers unsuccessfully tried to detain the "Poe Toaster," as he has come to be called, as he left the cemetery, but the man got away. Nothing like that has ever happened again.

After the note that was left in 1998, explaining that the "torch" had been passed to a new generation, witnesses reported a younger man was keeping up the tradition.

A note that was left in 2001 coincided with the Super Bowl that year, in which the Baltimore Ravens played the New York Giants. The note ended up stirring up controversy in Baltimore. It read: "The New York Giants. Darkness and decay and the big blue hold dominion over all. The Baltimore Ravens. A thousand injuries they will suffer. Edgar Allan Poe evermore."

The Toaster had never before commented on current events, so people were baffled by the negative reference to Baltimore's football team, which had been named in honor of Poe's most famous poem. The prophecy, a play on the last line of "The Masque of the Red Death," proved inaccurate, as Baltimore won the game 34-7.

In 2004, the Toaster's note was critical of France's opposition to the war in Iraq - "The sacred memory of Poe and his final resting place is no place for French cognac. With great reluctance but for respect for family tradition the cognac is placed. The memory of Poe shall live evermore!"

A final note - left sometime between 2005 and 2008 - was so dismaying that Jeff Jerome actually lied and publicly stated there had been no note. He has never revealed its contents, other than it was a hint that an end was coming to the tradition.

The original toaster - or at least his family - ended the tradition in 2009, which was the 200th anniversary of Poe's birth.

However, it didn't conclude before someone took responsibility for it. In 2007, a 92-year-old man named Sam Porpora claimed that he had started the tradition as a publicity stunt in the 1960s. He was the historian at Westminster Church at the time and he wanted to do something to reinvigorate the church and its congregation. His story, though, didn't really hold up. Published reports of the annual visits dated back to 1949, including an article in the *Sun* described "an anonymous citizen who creeps in annually to place an empty bottle (of excellent label) against the gravestone."

Porpora's daughter said that she'd never heard her father mention this before but that the story was consistent with his "mischievous nature." Nevertheless, Jeff Jerome pointed out that Porpora's story seemed to change every time he told it, so it was hard to take it seriously. He added, "There are holes so big in Sam's story, you could drive a Mack truck through them." Jeff Savoye of the Edgar Allan Poe Society also questioned Porpora's claims but admitted he couldn't definitively disprove them.

Porpora never retracted his story but later acknowledged that he might have inflated his role a bit. He never made the annual visits, he admitted. An unknown person had apparently made the tradition he invented their own.

In 2010, as Jeff Jerome expected, the Poe Toaster failed to appear. The following year saw only the appearance of four imposters - immediately dubbed "Faux Toasters." They were immediately labeled as fakes when they walked in clear sight of gathered observers, something the real Toaster never did. They also failed to give a secret signal that only Jerome knows and didn't arrange the roses in the unique pattern that the Toaster always used. The appearance of the four imposters sparked controversy - some preferred that the tradition die a "dignified death", while others urged that it be carried on, by imitators if necessary.

In 2012, the Toaster failed to appear again and this time, Jeff Jerome - who has always denied rumors that he was himself the Toaster - stated that the tradition had come to an end. As he told a reporter, "I would have thought they would leave a note for me saying it was over. That does annoy me a little bit, but they are under no obligation to do so."

But that, as is often said, was not the end of the story. In 2015, the Maryland Historical Society organized a committee to select a new "Poe Toaster" to carry on the annual tradition in a tourist-friendly manner. The new Toaster - who remains anonymous - made his first appearance during the daylight hours of January 16, 2016, which, being three days before Poe's birthday, but on a Saturday, was about as tourist-friendly as you can get.

But he wore the traditional garb and after playing Saint-Saëns' *Danse Macabre* on a violin, he raised a cognac toast and placed the roses. That marked a new, watered-down, non-mysterious tradition that continues today. It's not the same but at least the tradition is still alive, sort of anyway.

But no matter what's been done to weaken the tradition for our modern lives, the original mystery remains unsolved. Each year, on January 19, a mysterious man entered the burial ground and left his offering on the grave of one of America's greatest writers.

Who he was, no one will ever know.

And I believe that's for the best.

Some mysteries aren't meant to be solved.

10. Poe's Haunted History

EVEN IN THE GRAVE, ALL IS NOT LOST.
— EDGAR ALLAN POE

It wouldn't be true if I told you that the Westminster Burial Ground was the only place that laid claim to Edgar Allan Poe as its resident ghost. There are many places - Poe's old "haunts," if you will - where the spirit of the poet and writer is still said to linger.

Honestly, strange stories about Poe sprang up within days of his death. The oldest I could find concerned Poe's beloved pet cat, which was not black, by the way. The tortoiseshell cat that he'd named Catterina was at home with Maria Clemm when she learned that her "beloved Eddie" had died. The cat apparently just decided not to go on living. She died that very same day.

Poe in the Spirit World

As mentioned earlier, Sarah Helen Whitman - Poe's love interest and sort-of fiancé after Virginia's death and before he was engaged to Elmira Shelton - had a great interest in Spiritualism and in possible communication with Poe's ghost.

Interestingly, Sarah had been born in Providence, Rhode Island, on January 19, 1803 - exactly six years to the day before Poe. She later married the poet and writer John Winslow Whitman, the co-editor of the Boston Spectator and Ladies' Album, which allowed Sarah to publish some of her poetry using the name "Helen." John died in 1833; he and Sarah never had children.

Sarah Helen Whitman was so convinced that Poe was trying to communicate with her from beyond the grave that she hired a medium to live in her home full-time and wait for messages from Poe.

As a young widow, she became friends with intellectuals all over New England. She became interested in transcendentalism after hearing Ralph Waldo Emerson lecture in Boston, which in turn led to her interest in science, mesmerism, and the occult. She always wore black - long after her prescribed time of mourning for her husband was over - and wore a coffin-shaped charm around her neck. Is it any surprise that she became a great admirer of Poe?

Sarah and Poe first crossed paths in Providence in July 1845. Poe was attending a lecture by his friend and fellow poet, Fanny Osgood. After the lecture, Poe and Fanny passed by Sarah's house while she was standing in the rose garden behind the house. Poe declined to be introduced to her - he was infatuated with Fanny at the time - but it was enough for Sarah to simply see him. She was already an admirer of his stories and writings. As she admitted to her friend, Mary E. Hewitt:

> *I can never forget the impressions I felt in reading a story of his for the first time... I experienced a sensation of such intense horror that I dared neither*

look at anything he had written nor even utter his name... By degrees this terror took the character of fascination–I devoured with a half-reluctant and fearful avidity every line that fell from his pen.

A friend, Annie Lynch, asked Sarah to write a poem for a Valentine's Day gathering she was hosting in 1848 and Sarah agreed. She wrote the poem for Poe, even though he was not in attendance. He heard about the tribute, though, and returned the favor by anonymously sending his previously-printed poem "To Helen" to Sarah's home.

Sarah likely had no idea who had sent the poem, so she never responded. Three months later, Poe wrote her an entirely new poem, also called "To Helen," that referenced the moment from several years before when he had first seen Sarah in the rose garden behind her house.

It was what became a love affair with Sarah that led to his alleged suicide attempt after Virginia's death. He took two doses of laudanum, which caused him to become very sick and nearly die. Shortly after, he spent four days in Providence with her, his dismay apparently forgotten.

Though the two of them had many common interests, Poe was concerned about Sarah's friends, many of whom he had little regard and at least one - Elizabeth Ellet - that he grew to despise. Poe once wrote to her, "My heart is heavy, Helen, for I see that your friends are not my own."

The two of them exchanged letters and poetry for some time before they began discussing engagement. After Poe lectured in Providence in December 1848, reciting a poem by Edward Coote Pinkney directly to Sarah, she agreed to an "immediate marriage."

Poe vowed to Sarah that he would stay sober during their engagement - a promise that he broke within a few days. To make matters worse, Sarah's mother discovered that Poe had already asked several other women to marry him. Even so, the wedding came so close to taking place that, in January 1849, several newspapers announced their marriage and wished them well.

Sarah was barraged by criticisms about her relationship with Poe from friends and enemies alike. Sarah once received an anonymous letter that suggested Poe had broken his vow of sobriety in order to end their engagement. Poe blamed Sarah's mother for the letter. It was Rufus Griswold who eventually spread the story that Poe had purposely ended their relationship by getting drunk before the wedding so that Sarah would call it off. There may have been some truth to that part, but the rest was fiction. Griswold further claimed that Poe committed "unnamed drunken outrages that made necessary a summons of the police."

We will never know for certain why their engagement was broken off, but we do know that Sarah continued to think of Poe fondly for the rest of her life.

In 1860, Sarah published her first defense of Poe against the critics, namely Rufus Griswold, who had been spreading lies about him for more than a decade. A critic from a Baltimore newspaper said her book was a noble effort "but it does not wipe out the... dishonorable records in the biography of Dr. Griswold." Sarah also corresponded with Poe biographer John Ingram, hoping to set the record straight about the poet.

When Spiritualism became a popular movement around the country, Sarah openly embraced it and on Sundays, she practiced séances in her home, hoping to communicate with the dead - especially Poe. At one point in the 1860s, she was so convinced that Poe was trying to speak to her that she hired a professional medium to move into her home so that none of Poe's communications would be missed.

Sarah died at the age of 75 in 1878 at the home of a friend in Providence. In her will, she used the bulk of her estate to publish a volume of her own poetry and a volume for her sister.

When Sarah stepped beyond the veil, we can almost count on the fact that she hoped that Poe was waiting there to greet her.

Poetry After Death

Another woman who believed she had a direct line to Edgar Allan Poe was Elizabeth "Lizzie" Doten, a poet and prominent

Spiritualist lecturer, trance speaker, and writer who gained attention for her ability to channel poetry direct from the ghost of Poe himself.

Lizzie had been born into a prominent family in Plymouth, Massachusetts, in 1827. Both of her parents were Mayflower descendants and two of her brothers were officers during the Civil War. Another brother, Alfred, became a well-known writer and journalist in California and Nevada.

Lizzie Doten believed that she could channel the work of many dead writers, but most notably, she often heard from Edgar Allan Poe.

Lizzie was educated in public school before spending one year at a private academy at the age of 17. She was reported to have had psychic experiences as a child, leading to her lifelong interest in the occult and the supernatural. She also wrote poetry as a child, which combined with her interest in the spirit world, would have a great effect on her life.

As an adult, Lizzie began speaking about Spiritualism, advocating for the rights of spirit mediums, especially women. She became a champion for women's rights, equal pay for women, and often spoke out against marriage as a means of financial survival for women. She generally ended her lectures by reciting a poem - a poem that she claimed had been dictated from beyond the grave.

According to Lizzie, some of the poems in her two published books had been given to her by the spirits of several dead poets, but most notably by Edgar Allan Poe. This was a way, she said, for him to continue writing after death. She said that she would enter a trance and then the poems would come to her under the influence of the spirit. She spoke each aloud as she received them, and they were transcribed by an assistant. Needless to say, critics were skeptical and found it difficult to believe the poetry she published was the posthumous work of Poe.

Lizzie eventually retired from mediumship and public speaking for health reasons in 1880. In 1902, at the age of 75, she married her longtime companion, Z. Adams Willard, and moved to California for a few years. They eventually returned to Massachusetts, where Lizzie died in 1913 at the age of 85.

We can only wonder what the spirit of Poe the critic would have to say about the poems she had long been passing off as his work in the afterlife. I don't imagine his words were kind.

Poe Still Walks in Baltimore

The city of Baltimore has been called many things in the past, but the nicest one is "Charm City." It's a great town and its famous for its crab cakes, it's pubs, and Poe. This harbor city was once a thriving port in the 1700s and 1800s, and in many places, its grittiness has given way to gentrification, as long as you don't stray too far away from the bright lights and the beaten path.

There are many places to stay in Baltimore, especially around the touristy Inner Harbor area, but I always direct people toward Fell's Point, my favorite part of the city. It's here - in the original old Baltimore - that travelers can find pubs, seafood restaurants, and a lot of history. There are also some great hotels here, like the Sagamore Pendry, which opened in 2017 at the site of the once abandoned Recreation Pier. Fans of TV's "Homicide" series will still recognize the side door as the entrance to the show's police station.

On a nearby corner is the Admiral Fell Inn, which bears the name of William Fell, the sea captain who originally laid out port and watched it all turn into warehouses after the local shipbuilding industry declined. With its cobblestone streets and row houses, the Fells Point neighborhood is a city, state, and national historic district. Nowadays, it's lined with upscale shops, restaurants, and taverns, which have replaced transient sailors, busy brothels, and numerous saloons.

William Fell has likely seen it all - his ghost is still believed to haunt the inn that bears his name - but it's a place that Poe knew, too.

Just down the street is the world-famous Bertha's Mussels, a seafood spot that is known for its bright green bumper stickers that can be found all over the globe.

The Horse You Came In On Saloon on Fell's Point is located on the site of Ryan's Tavern, where some say Poe had his last drink. He was found in the gutter outside of the building. Today, the saloon claims that Poe's ghost makes frequent appearances.

This building is also haunted by a resident woman in black who makes frequent appearances and a little girl who has been spotted in the restaurant.

When asked, residents of Fell's Point can tell you that this is the most haunted part of town - and that certainly seems to be the case. Haunted pubs include Cat's Eye Pub, where things have a history of falling off the walls and moving around. The resident ghost is said to be "Giselle," a long-dead brothel madam, who is occasionally spotted around the place.

There's also The Whistling Oyster, which is known for phantom footsteps and inexplicable noises, and Friends Bar, which is home to unusual sounds like tinkling glasses and women's high-heeled shoes. Famous singer Billie Holliday once performed here and a drink is always left out for her each night on the bar, just in case she's one of the ghosts who frequents the place.

And then there's the pub that's of most interest to us within these pages - The Horse You Came In On saloon. It's a place with two noteworthy claims. One is that it claims to be the oldest operating bar in America and the other, that it was the last place Edgar Allan Poe had a drink.

It was in the gutter in front of this building in 1849 that Poe was discovered by Joseph Walker when it was still Ryan's Tavern. The owners and staff of this pub blame most of their eerie happenings on Poe's busy and well-traveled ghost. Manifestations reported include a swinging chandelier, a cash register that operates on its own, glasses and other bar items that move about, and bar stools that move on their own.

Poe's ghost - which must be tired from all the traveling - can rest for a bit at the Annabel Lee Tavern in Baltimore's Canton neighborhood. Named for Poe's last poem, it's the only Poe-themed restaurant and bar in the city. Guests are surrounded by stuffed ravens, scrawled Poe verses on the walls, and cocktails with names like "The Masque of Red Death." But it's unlikely you'll find any hauntings here.

The same might not be said for another Poe location in Baltimore - the Poe House and Museum, a cramped row house that was home to Poe, Virginia, and Maria Clemm in the 1830s. It's a place that really allows you to understand the poverty they suffered from during that time and, even today, the neighborhood around it is not one of the most inviting in Baltimore.

Decorated with period pieces - including a number of objects owned by Poe - it's a place well worth the visit. There are photos throughout the house, including a daguerreotype of Poe as a young man with no mustache. There is also a reproduction of a portrait of Poe's mother, a photograph of Maria Clemm, and a copy of the only portrait ever made of Virginia - an eerie, somber image that was painted just before her death.

But there may be more in this house than just remnants of Poe's life. Many visitors believe they feel a supernatural presence here, especially in Virginia's dark bedroom. Curator Jeff Jerome attributes this to the ambience and irregularities of the old house but has a hard time dismissing some of the other reports from guests.

Surprisingly, there are no claims that Poe himself haunts his former home. There have been many reports of an elderly woman

The Poe House and Museum in Baltimore is the cramped row house where Poe lived with Virginia and maria Clemm. It is allegedly haunted by spirits from the past, although not Poe himself.

who is seen in the bedrooms. She was, perhaps, a later resident of the house.

But there seems to be other spirits, too. Objects have been known to move around and guests have been touched by unseen hands on many occasions. Others have felt cold air brush by them in the crowded house on even the warmest days. Voices have been heard that have no explanation. Doors and windows open and close by themselves and the sounds of footsteps and thumps have been heard in various parts of the house.

Whoever the resident spirits might be, they seem to be aware they linger in the former home of one of the greatest horror writers in history and are doing what they can to make sure there's an eerie atmosphere about the place.

Lingering in Richmond

Located in downtown Richmond, Virginia, is a small stone house where Edgar Allan Poe never lived. Even so, visitors still gather here to pay respects to him. Many of the things that Poe cared for can be found within these walls, though, which is why some believe that his ghost may make an occasional appearance here, too.

Whether it is Poe who roams these halls or not, too many people have reported encounters at the Edgar Allan Poe Museum that they cannot explain. They are convinced, without a doubt, that the place is haunted.

The Poe Museum in Richmond is located in a small stone house that Poe
never lived in. However, it's believed that the relics that are stored here
have attracted the shadowy spirit of the writer himself, as well as other
haunts from the past.

The little stone house was built sometime around 1750 - the
exact date is a mystery - but in 1909 it gained local interest when a
group of concerned Richmond citizens petitioned the city
government to formally recognize the contributions of Edgar Allan
Poe. While their pleas to have a statue erected in his honor were
denied - because thanks to the efforts of Rufus Griswold he had long
been deemed "disreputable" - the city did start building a collection
of items that had once belonged to Poe. In 1911, the collection found
a home in the small stone house, which was located only a few blocks
from the Allan home, where Poe had grown up.

Soon after the collection was moved into the house, the
ghostly stories began. Whether the result of wild imaginations under
the influence of Poe, or legitimate happenings, there is now a history
of hauntings here that date back more than a century.

There are said to be at least three restless ghosts who haunt
the tiny house. The first two are a pair of blond children who are
believed to be part of the family who built the house. While they

have never been seen with the naked eye, they do have a habit of showing up in photographs that are taken by visitors. They tend to show up at random in wedding photos and candid snapshots. This has been happening for at least 30 years but, of course, the children never look any older.

The identity of the third ghost officially remains a mystery, but some of the visitors and staff believe that the shadowy figure is Poe himself. They believe he visits the place, still attached to some of the items that are displayed in the museum. One of them is the walking stick that he held behind in Richmond when he departed for Baltimore and the other is a hand mirror that once belonged to Virginia.

But whether the ghost is actually Poe, there's no denying that strange things happen here. They reported often, from footsteps to tapping sounds - like those at a "chamber door," I guess - and my favorite incident that occurred one night after the museum had closed. It seems that a shipment of Poe "bobble-heads" arrived just before closing and the boxes were left unopened on the floor to be dealt with the next morning. When the staff arrived, they found the box had been opened and unpacked and the figures had been lined up on a counter - without the museum's alarm being tripped.

"This Home of Horror Haunted!"

Hidden away in a park in Bronx, New York. is a small cottage that has defied the changes around it for more than 200 years - when Fordham was much different than it is today.

When Poe moved into this house in 1846, he was looking for a country house where Virginia could hopefully heal from the consumption that was destroying her. By then, Poe had already achieved fame and celebrity with stories and poems like "The Tell-Tale Heart" and "The Raven," but he still couldn't seem to make any money. By the time he moved to the Fordham area of what's now the Bronx, he'd already moved 18 times, doing everything he could to give Virginia the kind of life he felt she deserved, but he could never afford. This house seemed to be his last hope, especially at $5 a month for rent.

The cottage in the Bronx where Poe, Virginia, and Maria Clemm lived at the end of Virginia's life. She died in this house and some believe she has never left it.

He moved in with Virginia and Maria Clemm with high hopes that were soon shattered. Virginia's disease had gradually grown worse over the years, putting her on a downward spiral that began on the night when she was playing piano and, to Poe's horror, when she opened her mouth to sing, blood came out instead of music. "Her life was despaired of," he wrote later. "She recovered partially, and I again hoped. At the end of a year, the vessel broke again. I went through precisely the same scene. Then again – again. Each time I felt all the agonies of her death – and at each accession of the disorder I loved her more dearly and clung to her life with more desperate pertinacity. I became insane, with long intervals of horrible sanity."

It was hell on earth for the already neurotic Poe. Virginia was his world and as she became more ill, rumors spread throughout the city that both of them were dying. Poe himself became a physical wreck. When Virginia became too sick to walk, she was moved into a cramped upper bedroom. Poe carried her up and down a narrow staircase each day.

Virginia died in the house and her death sent Poe into a nightmare of depression, mania, and alcohol. Through it all, though, Poe kept writing - mostly because he had no choice. As one of his friends wrote, "He did not seem to care, after she was gone, whether he lived an hour, a day, a week or a year."

Poe's pain seeps through in the words of his 1849 memorial poem for her, "Annabel Lee," which has lines like:

I was a child and she was a child,
But we loved with a love that was more than love.
That the wind came out of the cloud by night,
Chilling and killing my Annabel Lee.

Poe visited Virginia's grave constantly. She had been entombed in their landlord's family crypt. His friend Charles Burr wrote, "Many times was he found at the dead hour of a winter night, sitting beside her tomb, almost frozen in the snow."

In the fall of 1849, Poe suffered his own untimely death, linking the two tragic figures forever.

Maria Clemm continued to live in the Fordham cottage for another 20 years. A visitor to Poe's house had earlier written, "The cottage had an air of taste and gentility... So neat, so poor, so unfurnished, and yet so charming a dwelling I never saw." But Maria survived by selling off the family valuables a piece at a time so she could eat.

She did manage to hang onto a few things, though, or at least someone did. The cottage today contains authentic period furnishings and three items that actually belonged to the Poe family - a rickety bed, a rocking chair, and a stained and cracked mirror with a gold frame.

And it's around these three items that the hauntings in the house center around.

The rocking chair has a pesky habit of rocking by itself, even when no one is around, the room is empty, and there are no suspicious breezes floating across the room.

The golden mirror has its own stories. It seems that Maria's spirit might be attached to it somehow. As a staff member at the site said during an interview, "His mother-in-law clearly held onto this mirror for a reason. It probably meant something very special." Over the years, a number of visitors have reported seeing the spectral face of a woman appear in the cracked glass, only to vanish when they looked closer. One guest even captured the face on video. It is Maria? No one can say for sure but it's certainly unsettling.

The gold mirror in the cottage, which some believe holds Maria Clemm's spirit in the house.

The old bed seems to have an attachment all its own - a mournful young woman that many believe may be Virginia Poe herself. There have been at least a dozen different reports of visitors who have entered the room where the bed is kept, only to see a woman in a dark dress scurry out of sight, as if afraid to get too close to them.

Below - Virginia's death bed. Some claim to have seen a young woman in a dark dress leave this room when early visitors enter it.

It should have been a house of sadness and, yet, Poe thought of the cottage as a place of joy - perhaps because it was where he spent the final days with Virginia. He wrote of the house as inspiration for his final story, the strangely serene "Landor's Cottage." And even Virginia described it as her dream house before she died, writing,

"Give me a cottage for my home and a rich old cypress vine, removed from the world. Love alone shall guide us when we are there."

And perhaps that's the reason she has never left.

Chasing Charleston's "Annabel Lee"

Ghostly legends abound in South Carolina and some of them involve Edgar Allan Poe. The only issue is that when those legends are mixed with fact, things become a bit of a mess. Historians say that there is no definitive record of Poe ever spending any time in Charleston, but it's possible - even plausible - that he visited the city during this military service at nearby Sullivan's Island. Poe later wrote of the year of boredom he spent at this post, so it's likely that he went into the city, looking for something to do.

If he didn't, well, as many Charleston residents say - "prove it." They maintain that travelers searching for traces of Poe can find them in South Carolina's coastal low country, from the islands to the city of Charleston itself.

One of the most famous sites in the region is tiny Sullivan's Island, which is only just over three miles square. It's a barrier island about nine miles north of Charleston's harbor and was once home to Fort Moultrie, which gained its fame in 1776 when commander William Moultrie kept British warships from invading Charleston during the American Revolution.

It was at Fort Moultrie where Poe - enlisted in the army under the name Edgar Perry - was stationed beginning in November 1827. He remained there for just over a year, he said, with very little to do.

Sullivan's Island did provide material for at least one of Poe's best stories, however - "The Gold Bug," a mystery story about a search for pirate's treasure. He didn't write the story while on the island, but it did provide the setting for the tale, which he published in 1843. But maybe not the entire setting, or at least that's what another location claims.

The sprawling Wild Dunes Resort, located on the Isle of Palms, is a huge waterfront playground with lodging, tennis courts, restaurants, a golf course. According to resort staffers, the golf course is situated on a piece of land that Poe often explored while staying at Fort Moultrie. They claim that a large oak tree that is located on the fairway of the 13th hole is the tree that appears in "The Gold Bug." If you've read the story, you know which tree they mean.

They also make the rather improbable claim that Poe's ghost is sometimes spotted out there near the tree.

As mentioned, a lot of the spirited tales of Poe in Charleston are a bit of a reach but none of them are as questionable as his ties to the ghost woman in white who haunts the Unitarian Church Graveyard in the city.

There are several large oak trees - at Wild Dunes Resort and on Sullivan's Island - that claim to be the "Gold Bug Tree." Since no one knows either way, we'll just use an illustration from the story...

Speculation and local lore claims that a young woman named Anna Ravenel, from an old, prominent Charleston family, became Poe's love during his time at Fort Moultrie. They also claim that she was the inspiration for his last published poem "Annabel Lee," even though every literary scholar around states that it was his wife, Virginia.

But that's the story I'm going to pass along now. I'm just doing my job here, passing along all of the "Poe ghost stories," whether they are silly or not. So, here goes this one:

The Unitarian Church Graveyard is home to the wildest Charleston ghost story connected to Edgar Allan Poe. But as many have said in the past, "Never let the truth get in the way of a good story."

The legend tells the story of this beautiful young woman, who was just 14-years-old when Poe was stationed near Charleston in 1827. She was the daughter of the most influential man in the city and engaged to be married to a young man from another prosperous family. But Anna fell in love with a soldier stationed at Fort Moultrie, an 18-year-old named Edgar Perry. He was instantly smitten by the smart, funny young woman.

When Anna's father realized that she had fallen for a soldier, he tried very hard to keep them separated. He tried locking Anna in the house and even tried sending thugs to warn Edgar away from seeing her. But the pair always found a way to be together, often arranging secret late-night meetings in a local cemetery.

In December 1828, Edgar was transferred away from Fort Moultrie, much to the relief of Anna's father. A short time later, though, Anna was stricken with a mysterious fever and became seriously ill. Her sister was able to get word to Edgar that Anna was sick but before he could return to her, she died. Edgar was devastated and journeyed back to Charleston for her funeral, only to be turned away by her family.

The story then goes on to say that Anna's father was determined to keep his daughter and Edgar apart - even in death. He purchased six plots in the Unitarian Church Cemetery - the same graveyard where the lovers secretly met - and buried Anna in one of them. He had the five other plots also dug up and then refilled so that Edgar would never be able to figure out which one was his beloved's grave.

Edgar was never able to pay his last respects to Anna, which he regretted for the rest of his life.

There are elements of truth to this story. The Ravenel family was real, and so was Anna. Poe was stationed at Fort Moultrie - under his pseudonym - from November 1827 to December 1828.

But the only connection that Poe actually had to anyone named Ravenel was to a man named Edmund Ravenel, who had a house on Sullivan Island near the fort. He was a conchologist, a study that Poe had an interest in, and the two men became friends.

And no, Anna was not Edmund Ravenel's daughter. He would have been only 16 when Anna was born. He did have a few older brothers but there were many branches to the Ravenel family tree and Edmund was the only one that Poe knew. Edmund went on to become one of the founders of the Medical University of South Carolina and it's likely that he was the inspiration for the character of William Legrand in Poe's story "The Gold Bug."

Anna Ravenel, however, was not the inspiration for "Annabel Lee," no matter what Charleston residents say.

Regardless of this, it is said that she still walks in the graveyard where she was buried. The Unitarian Church Cemetery is located on King Street in Charleston and its open to visitors during the day.

Anna's ghost, though, shows up at night, around the time when she and Edgar allegedly met. She continues to make appearances around her still-unmarked grave, searching for the love that changed her life. She has been seen walking, or sitting on a nearby bench, looking about anxiously for the spirit of Edgar Allan Poe - a man she undoubtedly never met.

Legends can be a funny thing, can't they?

Poe at Fort Monroe

In December 1828, Poe - still known as Edgar Perry - was transferred away from Charleston to Fort Monroe, new Hampton, Virginia.

By that time, construction on the fort wasn't quite finished. There had been a foundation in place at the site for years, but it was fortified during the War of 1812, when the United States was forced to establish a coastal defense system to fend off the British. After the embarrassing incident during which British troops invaded Washington, D.C. and burned the White House, new forts were quickly established.

Fort Monroe was armed with nearly 200 cannons, controlling the channel that led directly to the capital.

When Poe arrived at Fort Monroe, he was given a promotion and a new job, which involved preparing artillery shells for those cannons. During his time here he was promoted to the rank of sergeant major but also learned to despise the drudgery of the army - which makes it odd that he allegedly still visits this place in the afterlife.

But if Poe does walk here, he doesn't walk alone.

Most of the fort's infamy came during the years of the Civil War, when its armaments and defenses were improved to protect it from possible Confederate attack. Considered the "Gibraltar of Chesapeake Bay," Fort Monroe served as the starting point of several land operations against the Confederate Army and was so impregnable that it was one of the few Southern forts not captured by the Confederacy during the war. For this reason, President Lincoln didn't hesitate to visit the fort in May 1862 to help plan the attack on Norfolk. In 1864, General Ulysses S. Grant stayed at Fort Monroe while he helped prepare the plans that brought about the end of the war.

During World War II, Fort Monroe bristled with an impressive complement of coastal artillery guns, long-range cannons, and a series of rapid-fire weapons. Many of these advances in weapons technology were soon obsolete when the potential of the long-rang bomber and aircraft carrier was realized at the end of

A vintage painting of Fort Monroe as it would have looked during the time that Poe was stationed there.

the war. Today, Fort Monroe serves as the headquarters for the U.S. Army Training and Doctrine Command.

In addition to still serving as a military post, it is also a very haunted place. There have been reports of military apparitions, the phantom clumping of boots, rustling of phantom skirts, the sound of disembodied laughter, and the ghosts of several famous people, including General Grant and Abraham Lincoln. The former president has been spotted many times in the plantation-style home called Old Quarters Number 1, clad in a dressing gown and standing deep in thought by the fireplace of the appropriately named Lincoln Room.

And, of course, there is one other specter here who is frequently reported in his former barracks, Building No. 5 - Edgar Perry, who was of course Edgar Allan Poe. He served four months at Fort Monroe before he sold his enlistment to a man who was never completely paid for it.

If Poe was here for such a short time - and likely hated every minute of it - then what would make his spirit linger behind? Perhaps it's more for literary reasons than for any sort of unfinished business. During this time in Building No. 5, Poe is said to have

The steps leading down into the dungeon that helped to inspire the story "The Cask of Amontillado."

gotten the idea for his story, "The Cask of Amontillado." There was a ghost story already told about a soldier who had been walled up alive inside the building. Poe took the general notes of the story - set it in the dungeon that was located at Fort Independence in Boston, his first posting - - and created an original tale of murder and revenge.

Is that reason enough for him to return again and again to the old barracks after death? Not in my opinion, but I suppose we'll never know for sure. Legend has it that he's here, so you'll have to judge the validity of the tale for yourself.

Epilogue

THERE IS NO EXQUISITE BEAUTY... WITHOUT SOME STRANGENESS IN THE PROPORTION.
– EDGAR ALLAN POE

What else can I say about Poe that I haven't already said? As I've already made clear, I have long been fascinated with the author, especially with the mystery of his final days. I'm not alone in my fascination, of course.

Poe is what I always thought of as entry-level "goth" in my younger days. For kids I knew who wanted to stretch their legs into the macabre and yet had strict parents who wouldn't approve of mascara, dyed-black hair, morbid outfits, facial piercings, and The Cure, Poe was safe. It seemed literary and smart, but it also opened the door to the dark side for a couple of generations of us who grew up in the 1980s and 1990s. I suppose he's still offering that same escape to many people today.

And he's offered so much more to the world of literature and horror as a whole, likely more than anyone - except for perhaps Poe himself, who recognized his own genius, even when no one else did - during his time could have imagined.

`

Jules Verne, Sir Arthur Conan Doyle, and Stephen King all admitted the influence that Poe had on their work. "He wasn't just a mystery/suspense writer," wrote the author many fans would describe as the modern Poe, Stephen King. "He was the first."

Poe lived most of his life in abject poverty, keeping food on the table and a roof over his head the only way he knew - by writing. After self-publishing his first books of poetry, which vanished without leaving so much of a ripple behind), he began selling stories to magazines, newspapers, and journals. That led him to jobs as editor and critic, which allowed him to get some of his stories into print.

Even though Poe heavily influenced horror, many of his stories weren't about the supernatural. Instead, they often took a psychological approach to stories of crime and tragedy that were far afraid of their time. Poe was simply obsessed with being obsessed - ripping a page from his own life. "The Black Cat" and "The Tell-Tale Heart" are both narrated by psychotic killers driven to destroy themselves by guilt-fueled hallucinations. In "The Oval Portrait," an artist becomes so fixated on finishing a painting, he doesn't even notice that his beautiful model–his wife–is dead. And even "The Fall of the House of Usher" isn't a ghost story, even if many of us remember it that way - often thanks to Vincent Price and Roger Corman's Poe films. It's the story of a twisted, quasi-incestuous relationship between a young woman and the brother who tries to have her interred alive.

Of course, Poe wasn't the only writer who was cranking out dark tales of horror and murder in those days. The era of the "penny dreadful" had arrived and there was plenty of paper being devoted to blood-soaked shockers. And yes, Poe stood apart from his rivals, largely because of his emphasis on the aberrant psychology that he was so familiar with and, of course, because his imagination was far greater than anyone else writing at the time.

Poe was not just pushing the envelope of genres that already existed, he was creating new ones. With his story "The Murders in the Rue Morgue," he created the mystery. He did what no other writer had yet thought to do - took the intellectual challenge of the puzzles and ciphers he loved so much and used them as the hook for a work of fiction.

"To Poe," wrote Sir Arthur Conan Doyle, the creator of Sherlock Holmes, "must be ascribed the monstrous progeny of writers on the detection of crime. Each may find some little development of his own, but his main art must trace back to those admirable stories of Monsieur Dupin." Doyle later added, "Poe is the master of all."

Doyle wrote these words praising Poe in the late nineteenth century. Stephen King also praised Poe nearly a century later, but such high praise would have come as a surprise to the writers and critics of Poe's own era, since to them it appeared that Poe was the master of nothing, except perhaps living shamefully and dying young.

As we know from earlier pages in this book, Poe was never rich nor even really famous. He had a bad habit of squandering every chance that he had to make his life better. His erratic behavior, literary feuds, and vicious reviews wrecked his career, and his murky death became the last proverbial nail in the coffin of his reputation.

And then after his death, his literary legacy died, too, thanks to Rufus Griswold. As discussed, he did everything he could to destroy Poe, lying about his school and army careers, his addictions, and even his sanity. He altered Poe's letters to make them look more hateful and more slanderous and then made sure that Maria Clemm was cheated out of any money made from publications of Poe's posthumous works. It was not only a horrific, tireless crusade against Poe, it was a successful one. Poe was considered morally reprehensible, and his work was not considered a suitable model for American literature for at least 50 years.

In France, though, Poe's reputation as an opium-addled madman probably helped. The French poet Charles Baudelaire worshipped Poe, seeing in him not only a kindred spirit but a victim of delusional critics with very sharp pens. Poe was, to him, the classic misunderstood genius. Baudelaire set out to right that wrong by praising Poe to anyone who'd listen and translating the writer's tales into French. He became Poe's greatest press agent, painting the picture of Poe as rebellious and decadent, which is what appeals to so many people today. As a result, Poe was regarded as a master in France long before his reputation was salvaged at home.

When Poe was remembered in the United States - which wasn't by many - it was as a wild-eyed lunatic tortured by demons of his own creation. Which is, I believe, is the appeal that he has for so many young people who are first dipping their toes into the dark side. This gothic, larger-than-life persona meshed perfectly with Poe's dark tales, and it eventually gave him a sort of romantic glamour he didn't actually have when he was alive.

This mystique didn't just allow Poe's works to live on - it's kept Poe himself alive. He's become a living, breathing character in both fiction and non-fiction over the years, causing us to believe we know more of his secrets than we really do. Believe me when I say that despite my many years of fascination with Poe, I was constantly surprised when working on this book.

Poe finally began to get his due by the end of the nineteenth century. Not only were his contributions being acknowledged by Conan Doyle, the man who'd picked up the detective fiction torch he'd lit, but Poe also had a host of other high-profile champions, including W.H. Auden, H.G. Wells, Fyodor Dostoevsky, and George Bernard Shaw.

By the middle of the nineteenth century, Poe wasn't just famous, he was respectable enough to show up on high school reading lists alongside Twain, Melville, Hawthorne, Hemingway, and other authors who've shaped American literature. Of course, that was no guarantee of immortality -- thanks to the lack of enthusiasm most high school students bring to reading assignments - but Poe usually turns out to be the assigned reading that many students don't hate. They still stand up today and are as readable now as they were to the fans Poe had during his lifetime.

And Poe will live on. His life and works are still embraced by the student in the high school class who always wears black, the reader fascinated by the macabre, the budding horror writer, the seeker of original mystery tales, and people probably a lot like you and me - by anyone fascinated by the strange, the unusual, the haunted, and the unsolved.

Troy Allan Taylor
Spring 2021

Bibliography

Ackroyd, Peter - *Poe: A Life Cut Short*, London, Chatto & Windus, 2008

Allen, Hervey - *Israfel: The Life and Times of Edgar Allan Poe*, New York, Farrar & Rinehart, 1934

Asburt, Herbert - *All Around the Town*, New York, NY, Alfred A. Knopf, 1929
------------------ *Gem of the Prairie*, New York, NY, Alfred A. Knopf, 1940

Carter, John F., M.D. - "Edgar Poe's Last Night in Richmond" *Lippincott's Monthly Magazine*, November 1902

Barton, Steve - "Cold Spots: The Edgar Allan Poe Museum," *Dread Central*, 2009

Bittner, William - *Poe: A Biography*. Boston, MA, Little, Brown and Company, 1962

Dowdy, C. - "Poe's Last Visit to Richmond," *American Heritage*, March 1954

Eaves, T. - "Poe's Last Visit to Philadelphia," *American Heritage*, March 1954

Foye, Raymond, editor - *The Unknown Poe*, San Francisco, CA, City Lights. 1980

Geiling, Natasha - "The Still Mysterious Death of Edgar Allan Poe," *Smithsonian*, October 2014

Harrison, James A. - *A Life of Edgar Allan Poe*, New York, NY, Haskell House, 1970

Hockensmith, Steve - Evermore: The Enduring Influence of Edgar Allan Poe, *Mystery Scene*

Hoffman, Daniel -- *Poe Poe Poe Poe Poe Poe Poe*. Baton Rouge, LA, Louisiana State University Press, 1972

Ingraham, J.H. - *The Beautiful Cigar Girl, or Mysteries of Broadway*, New York, NY, Robert M. De Witt, 1844

Ingram, John H. - *Edgar Allan Poe*, London, John Hogg, 1880

Kennedy, J. Gerald, Editor - *A Historical Guide to Edgar Allan Poe*, Oxford, Oxford University Press, 2001

Knapp, Francky - "Edgar Allan Poe's Cottage is Just Sitting There in the Bronx," October 2018

Krutch, Joseph Wood - *Edgar Allan Poe: A Study in Genius*, New York, NY, Alfred A. Knopf, 1926

Lake, Matt - *Weird Maryland*, New York, NY, Sterling Publishing, 2006

Lavriere, Emile - *The Strange Life and Strange Loves of Edgar Allan Poe*, Philadelphia, PA, J.B. Lippincott Co., 1935

Lenoir, Andrew - "The Unsolved Murder That Fascinated 1840s New York (and Edgar Allan Poe)", *Mental Floss*, February 2017

Meyers, Jeffrey -- *Edgar Allan Poe: His Life and Legacy*, New York, NY, Cooper Square Press, 1992

Ocker, J.W. - *Poe-Land*, Woodstock, VT, Countryman Press, 2015

Okonowicz, Ed - *Big Book of Maryland Ghost Stories*, Guilford, CT, Globe Pequot, 2010

Porges, Irwin - *Edgar Allan Poe*, Philadelphia, PA, Chilton Books, 1963

Semter, Christopher - "13 Haunting Facts about Edgar Allan Poe's Death," *Biography*, October 2020
------------------------- - *Edgar Allan Poe's Richmond: The Raven in the River City*, Charleston, SC, History Press, 2012

Silverman, Kenneth - *Edgar A. Poe: Mournful and Never-Ending Remembrance*, New York, NY, Harper Collins, 1991

Sova, Dawn B. - *Edgar Allan Poe A to Z*, New York, NY, Checkmark Books, 2001

Srebnick, Amy Gilman -- *The Mysterious Death of Mary Rogers*, London, Oxford University Press, 1995

Standard, Mary Newton - *The Dreamer: A Romantic Rendering of the Life Story of Edgar Allan Poe*, Philadelphia, PA, J.B. Lippincott, 1925

Stashower, Daniel - *The Beautiful Cigar Girl*, New York, NY, Dutton, 2006

Symons, Julian - *The Tell-Tale Heart: The Life and Works of Edgar Allan Poe*, New York, NY, Harper & Row, 1978

Walsh, John Evangelist - *Midnight Dreary: The Mysterious Death of Edgar Allan Poe*, New Brunswick, NJ, Rutger University Press, 1998
---------------------------- - *Poe the Detective: The Curious Circumstances Behind the "Mystery of Marie Roget,"* New Brunswick, NJ, Rutgers University Press, 1968

-------------------------- - *Plumes in the Dust: The Love Affair of Edgar Allan Poe and Fanny Osgood*, Chicago, IL, Nelson Hall, 1981

Wimsatt, William K., Jr. - *Poe and the Mystery of Mary Rogers*, New York, NY, Modern Language Association of America, 1941

Winwar, Frances - *The Haunted Palace: A Life of Edgar Allan Poe*, New York, NY, Harper & Row, 1959

Woodberry, George E. - *The Life of Edgar Allan Poe*, New York, NY, Biblio & Tannen, 1965

Special Thanks to

April Slaughter: Cover Design and Artwork
Lois Taylor: Editing and Proofreading
Lisa Taylor and Lux
Orrin Taylor
Rene Kruse
Rachael Horath
Elyse and Thomas Reihner
Bethany Horath
John Winterbauer
Kaylan Schardan
Maggie and Packy Lundholm
Cody Beck
Becky Ray
Tom and Michelle Bonadurer
Lydia Roades
Susan Kelly and Amy Bouyear
Cheryl Stamp and Sheryel Williams-Staab
And the entire crew of American Hauntings

About the Author

Troy Taylor is the author of books on ghosts, hauntings, true crime, the unexplained, and the supernatural in America. He is also the founder of American Hauntings Ink, which offers books, ghost tours, events, and weekend excursions. He was born and raised in the Midwest and currently divides his time between Illinois and the far-flung reaches of America.

CPSIA information can be obtained
at www.ICGtesting.com
Printed in the USA
JSHW012125050623
42767JS00001B/24

9 781735 270654